Marketing with Smart Machines

Marketing with Smart Machines

Customer Interaction in the Algorithmic Economy

Alexander Borek and Joerg Reinold

Marketing with Smart Machines: Customer Interaction in the Algorithmic Economy, First Edition

Authors: Alexander Borek and Joerg Reinold

Development Editor: Laura Monroe
Technical Editor: Thomas C. Redman

ISBN-13: 9781530554355
ISBN-10: 1530554357
Library of Congress Control Number: 2016905781
CreateSpace Independent Publishing Platform
North Charleston, South Carolina
BISAC: Business & Economics / Marketing / General

Executing Digital Publishing, Berlin

For more information visit our website at www.executingdigital.com.

About this Book

The age of the intelligent machine is upon us, and with it comes a wealth of commercial opportunities for marketing managers willing to embrace cognitive technology and the algorithmic economy.

As the Internet of things continues to grow, wearable devices, smart-phones, and sensors provide Smart Machines with an omnipresent view-point. Factor in the deep learning capabilities of cognitive computing and automation, and the Smart Machine emerges as a powerful new force in commercial marketing—one capable of fundamentally changing the marketing landscape.

Innovative start-ups already capitalize on the power of Smart Machines. Established businesses need to adapt to remain competitive. *Marketing with Smart Machines* offers a guide to the powerful new marketing opportunities provided by the thinking machine.

About the Authors

Alexander Borek is responsible for Marketing Science, Smart Data & Analytics in the group digitalization of the twelve automotive brands of Volkswagen AG. He consulted at Gartner and IBM, advising Fortune Global

500 executives across multiple industries regarding digital transformation and analytics innovation strategies. He is an affiliated faculty member of the Information Quality Graduate Program at the University of Arkansas, Little Rock, and holds a PhD from the University of Cambridge, England.

Joerg Reinold leads the global industry solutions for IBM's Watson and commerce business within the media and entertainment industry. He built up IBM's international commerce consulting and software business and consulted within IBM's strategy and transformation practice. A member of IBM's commerce experts, Reinold is a keynote speaker and author of articles on digital and shared economy topics.

More Praise for *Marketing with Smart Machines: Customer Interaction in the Algorithmic Economy*

Alex and Joerg have created a bold vision: the Smart Machine as an up-and-coming competitive differentiator, something long understood and well applied by the Internet giants. They do a great job of introducing their vision in the modern marketplace and in explaining to nontechies what a Smart Machine is and how it works. Their practical breakdown of how the smart marketing executive can prepare for the future of Smart Machine marketing was very insightful. A must read for the marketing professional that aims to evolve in a world where a business's control over data is key to success.

—STAN CHRISTIAENS, COFOUNDER AND CTO, COLLIBRA

Borek and Reinold very ably highlight the disruptive power of the algorithmic economy and give the reader a glimpse of what the future will look like, making the case that much of the future is already here. They masterfully use simple analogies to highlight the powerful concepts of cognitive computing and pepper this book with great examples from real-use cases. They provide a simple road map and actionable advice on further transforming marketing, which I am certain will make this a handbook on contemporary marketing in an intelligent, interconnected, and instrumented world.

—PROFESSOR ANDY KORONIOS, HEAD, SCHOOL OF INFORMATION TECHNOLOGY AND MATHEMATICAL SCIENCES, UNIVERSITY OF SOUTH AUSTRALIA

What a fascinating book! It's amazing to think of all the opportunities these new smart technologies offer for the marketing world. The authors did a great job in making complex technological concepts easy to understand for business managers.

—MARKUS HELFERT, DIRECTOR, BUSINESS INFORMATICS GROUP, DUBLIN CITY UNVIERSITY

Smart Machines will do to marketing what automation did to logistics, manufacturing, and finance. Marketing needs a new operating model to deal with a new dimension of exponential complexity, speed, and also opportunity. Getting a systematic overview und understanding the new battlefield of marketing is definitely the first and best move to stay in and ahead of the game.

—DIRK JEHMLICH, MANAGING DIRECTOR, DIFFFERENT STRATEGIEAGENTUR GMBH

Many have heralded the age of the Smart Machine, but no one has really conceptualized what that means to marketers the way Borek and Reinold have in their new book. They describe how Smart Machines will—in practice—enable the fully personalized, one-to-one marketing approach and the customer-centric organizations we have been talking about for the last decade.

—BASTIAN LATT, DIRECTOR, ECCELERATE GMBH ECOMMERCE CONSULTING

If you're a marketing manager and haven't read this book, get nervous. Your peers will be smarter.

—ALEXANDER BROJ, PARTNER, DIGITAL
TRANSFORMATION AT BEARINGPOINT

Contents

Alexander Borek and Joerg Reinold

Foreword

On my first read of Alex and Joerg's book, I kept good notes and sent them off three pages full of tough questions. Why, I wondered, should one believe that artificial intelligence had finally arrived, after thirty years of hype? Or why would any socially conscious company embrace the age of algorithms if all it promises is lost jobs? And how does one square the notion that digital technologies fundamentally change the way we live with the decidedly less expansive views of Robert Gordon? My questions were tough and covered a lot of territory. There was no way Alex and Joerg could address them all.

But from another perspective, my questions missed the point. Most can agree that

* digital technologies offer new ways to communicate in all directions with customers;
* devices (call them the Internet of things or smart, connected devices) are already creating more and different data on a scale unimaginable just a few years ago, with no end in sight;
* more and more "work," once the exclusive province of humans, is being automated, again with no end in sight;
* today's organizations are "unfit for data," essentially unprepared for any of this; and

*   marketing is a "target-rich environment." After all, John Wanamaker (or maybe Henry Ford or J. C. Penney) observed perhaps one hundred years ago, "I know half of my advertising budget is wasted. The trouble is I don't know which half." Uncertainty in the attribution aside, the situation has hardly changed.

I hope your resounding answer to the above is *I agree*! So the really important questions for marketing are, what comes next week, in the not-too-distant future, and in the longer term?

This is where Alex and Joerg's book comes in. It provides an answer, covering the waterfront, bringing us up to date on these topics, and sketching a view of what can be. You'll find it easy to object to specific points, as I did. But you ignore the overall themes at your peril.

So I recommend you read this book on three levels. First, give it a fast read.

Alex and Joerg are unbridled optimists. You should let their enthusiasm help you dream big. There is a lot in the news these days about self-driving cars, a development I look forward to. But I hadn't thought much about how I'll use the time. After reading this book, I had dozens of new ideas, many of which present new opportunities to sell me stuff! Let your mind go in all directions in considering every aspect of your relationship with prospects and customers, whom you'll work with, the products you'll offer, and how you'll manage.

Next, return to today's reality. About a week later, pick the book up again and mull over the main points in the context of your current job. Then pick it up again, reading more carefully this time, and search for two ideas you want to put into practice. Give one a good try, learn from it, and then put the second idea into practice.

But, as Alex and Joerg make clear, you should do so with some care. It is all too easy to get caught up in the day-to-day frenzy, direct all one's attention to the short term, and then be caught unaware. From where I sit, most companies are still sorting out how to use e-mail, among the oldest digital marketing technologies, effectively. Let me cite one example. Last holiday season I purchased three items for my wife at one of her favorite retailers. Later that day, I talked to my wife, and she noted that she had to call that retailer. Evidently they had sent her an e-mail advising her of charges at the store. "Looks like some pretty good stuff," she observed, "but I didn't buy it."

Of course I had no choice but to reveal my shopping spree and spoil the surprise. The two of us worked out that she had joined some sort of frequent shopper club and that e-mailing her receipts was part of that program. In this case, they appear to have linked the credit card I used with her shopper club ID and sent the receipt along. Evidently it didn't occur to them that a couple could share a credit card account. Is this any way to build a trusting relationship? Seems like a rookie mistake to me.

After you've gained some experience, read this book a third time, with the goal of developing a more holistic, top-down plan. I'd like to tell you that Alex and Joerg offer a tried and true road map to the future. But that is certainly not the case. Such road maps do not exist, and I suspect that by the time they do, it will be too late. Way too late! This is the work for clear-eyed realists. Your plan must factor in the dynamics and specifics of your industry, your goals, and the human skills you can acquire, nurture, and grow. There is no free lunch here.

Finally, read Alex and Joerg's book "between the lines." The future that Alex and Joerg describe is not so much a destination as it is a journey. Even if you've mastered all there is to know about Smart Machines, the Internet of things, and customer engagement, something new will come along—and pretty darn soon.

So a component of your plan must specify those areas where you wish to be on the "bleeding edge," where you wish to be a "fast adopter," and where you wish to be "in the middle of the pack." Another component must clarify how you will test new ideas, develop them, and integrate them into your mix.

You're probably thinking, "Wow, you're asking a lot. How will we fit it all in?"

My counter is this: "What exactly is your alternative?"

After all, marketing departments are being assailed from all sides. One hour you are worried about the quality of contact data, the next you have a discussion of the implications of cloud computing, and on and on. This is not going to stop. While there is no guarantee of success, your best hope lies in understanding the overall landscape (by reading and rereading Alex and Joerg's book), understanding the landscape as it applies to your particulars (by trying out the ideas), and pulling all this together into a plan. At the very least, those attempting to make their own futures will have more fun!

Thomas C. Redman
"The Data Doc"
Rumson, NJ
USA
May 27, 2016

Chapter 1

* * *

Introduction to Smart Machines and the Algorithmic Economy

***All things must change to something
new, to something strange.***

—HENRY WADSWORTH LONGFELLOW

The Algorithmic Economy Is Coming

We are at the brink of another fundamental technological revolution. Computers beat humans in chess and the even more complex game of Go; they drive cars autonomously and give advice to doctors. Some of us saw IBM Watson winning against the all-time champions of *Jeopardy!* (a quiz game that requires deep understanding of natural language and a widespread knowledge of literature, music, art, politics, history, and many other domains). Already today, Smart Machines have become artists themselves, creating poems, news articles, music, and paintings that can compete with those produced by humans.

Smart Machines will soon become omnipresent through sensors and the Internet of things. The advancements in cognitive technologies enable them to think and learn by themselves, and increasingly they'll also make and execute decisions autonomously. Artificial intelligence is becoming more publicly available from a growing number of vendors to be used commercially across all industries. Algorithms will drive the future of our economy and will change the rules of the way we interact with our customers.

* Gartner defines algorithmic business as the industrialized use of complex mathematical algorithms pivotal to driving improved business decisions or process automation for competitive differentiation.[1]

Android robots and artificial intelligence have always been an important element of science fiction. In 2014 MIT researchers Erik Brynjolfsson and Andrew McAfee announced the "second machine age," which will impact the entire economy as much as the first machine age did with the invention of the steam engine and which will transform most of today's professions.[2] The algorithmic economy will soon become reality, when algorithms will be the most important competitive advantage for any industry. The algorithmic economy is driven by Smart Machines being able to capture nearly anything that happens in the physical world. These Smart Machines will become cognitive, increasingly understanding the meaning of data, text, images, and speech, and will enter one of the last frontiers of the human mind—our creativity. Watch out for machines writing poems, composing music, and creating paintings. Additionally, Smart Machines will make autonomous decisions with no human intervention, sometimes even literally in the driver's seat, as in the case of self-driving cars.

* The core idea of the algorithmic economy is that the competitive advantage in most industries will be driven by the intellectual property of smart algorithms.

A History of Disruption Continues with the Next Big Wave

It all started in 1995, when Amazon launched its first online shopping site. At that time, not too many people would have imagined that this new start-up could become the world's biggest retailer within twenty years. In 2001 the music industry was disrupted. The "Big Four," Universal, Sony, EMI, and Warner, hesitated to sell their music online, so Apple Inc. suddenly launched iTunes and out of nowhere became the number one retailer in the music industry (and has kept its pole position since then). Television channels saw their biggest threat in Netflix, founded in 1997, which allows consumers to watch the TV shows and movies of their choice whenever they want online. This has endangered the future of large media giants such as ABC, CBS, and NBC. All three of these examples describe new companies that used digital channels to provide traditional content when the traditional providers hesitated to use the new online channel. So far, digitization has disrupted those industries for which the Internet has opened up a new sales channel.

One company alone, namely Google, is already causing a lot of disturbances. When business leaders of car manufacturers see Google experimenting with self-driving vehicles, they ask themselves, "Will a car be still a car in the future, or will it be a large moving computer and data center?" Business leaders of insurance companies are concerned over how Google has captured a large percentage of the net profit of many insurance products in the United States and is experimenting with its own price-comparison site. Business leaders of household appliance manufacturers know they have to battle directly with Google to win the smart-home game after Google's $3.2 billion acquisition of Nest, a company that manufactures, among other things, a home thermostat that uses sensors to train itself according to a household's comings and goings.

Today we are entering another wave of digitization with Smart Machines that will not stop at any industry. When we spoke to top executives of incumbent leaders in traditional industries such as banking, insurance, consumer products, and manufacturing, they all admitted that the biggest threat to their companies' futures were digital-savvy companies and new technology start-ups from Silicon Valley and other innovation hubs. CEOs have carefully observed how new digital players have exiled established players in the retail, music, and TV industries, and they fear the same will happen to them. The algorithmic economy will impact every part of our lives through the new mobile channel, social media, and the Internet of things (where sensors and chips are hidden in traditional products).

Merging Physical and Digital Experiences

The world is changing rapidly and becoming digital. Digital technologies fundamentally change how we live, work, and interact and will also transform the basis of competition in most industries. This can make "the physical world better, worse, or just different," as Eric Schmidt and Jared Cohen of Google describe it.[3] The physical world is becoming rapidly more interconnected and interwoven with the physical world. As a result, the digital and real worlds are merging. Customers get messages and interact with companies on a multiplicity of channels: traditional physical branches, online shops, mobile, direct mail, phone, TV, e-mail, chat, digital marketing, social networks, blogs, and tweets, just to name a few. Shifting customer touch points and rising expectations for a better experience put pressure on marketing divisions to reinvent themselves.

> ★ With mobile phones, sensors, the Internet of things, wearable devices, the Internet, and the use of touch screens in shops, we see an increasing digitization of the physical world.

Customers expect the seamless digital experience that they know from digital giants like Google, Facebook, Amazon, Apple, and innovative start-ups. Traditional companies are struggling to provide the same quality of digital customer experience and leave room for new entrants. At this time, the revolution does not stop at digitizing a sales channel. It is about transforming the entire business model and using data and algorithms to provide a better and/or cheaper service or product.

When Science Fiction Turns Science Fact

We are entering a new era when science fiction is becoming science fact. Having all the information about the world as digital data allows computers to analyze this data with speed, precision, and context awareness and provides a new source of intelligence and automation. Since a large proportion of the whole planet will be equipped and interconnected with smartphones and integrated mobile computing devices at home and everywhere else in the not-too-far-off future, this new intelligence will be fully integrated into our lives.

* ★ Those robots we know from science fiction movies are entering our lives. Virtual and augmented reality are becoming mainstream.

The usage of digital data will become more and more intuitive. Wearable devices like Google Glass fully integrate into our environment. Mobile technologies and touch screens are increasingly used more than computers. In the future, we will be able to use computing devices in nearly the same natural way as we interact with other humans. Here again, voice recognition will become the key, along with natural language recognition. Making computers understand humans better is the next frontier of computing. And we see how this trend has already started with technologies like Apple's Siri, which is available on every iPhone and iPad as part of the iOS system. (A similar technology is available on Google Android and in other operating systems.) We can dictate an e-mail, ask what the weather is like, and change an appointment with a friend by simply talking to our phones. We can talk to our household appliances, our TVs, our cars, and our computers using natural language. With devices like the Xbox Kinect, everyday use of gesture-recognition technology is also on the rise. In the future, with one flick of the hand, we will be able to change the lighting, temperature, music track, and TV channel in the house, or in Schmidt and Cohen's words: "Your apartment is an electronic orchestra, and you are the conductor."[4]

★ The algorithms for artificial intelligence that are used by Smart Machines have been around for years. What has changed is the computing power available that finally allows one to apply the algorithms on a large scale.

More and more, this allows artificial intelligence to enter our normal lives. Imagine cars that can drive without a human driver, that can "see" the road and communicate with other cars to synchronize their movement. In California these cars are already in practical daily use. Household cleaning too will be increasingly performed by household robots. The robotic vacuum is only the beginning.

Over the past hundred years, we've automated many manual tasks. There is an ongoing trend indicating that this will be applied to other tasks that traditionally relied heavily on human thinking. Until today, doctors made diagnoses and determined treatments that are given to patients. But a new generation of computers like the IBM Watson is able to perform these tasks for the doctor based on the newest knowledge and insights gathered from all medical research available. Will this technology completely replace doctors soon? Probably not. But it will certainly allow doctors to perform remote surgeries and improve the quality of treatment.

* "By 2018, 50 percent of the fastest-growing companies will have fewer employees than instances of Smart Machines."[5]

What Makes a Machine Smart Are Algorithms and Data

The reason why Smart Machines are so much more powerful than conventional computer programs are the advanced AI (artificial intelligence) algorithms and the data they can absorb. Smart Machines can sense their own state and environment and can communicate with other Smart Machines. They are self-learning and can solve very complex problems, and they can act, sometimes autonomously. There are many technologies behind the capabilities of Smart Machines. The most important enabler is the massive amount of computing power and storage that is available today for a relatively cheap price, which makes it finally possible to apply computational heavy artificial intelligence algorithms that would have not been possible some years ago.

* Smart Machines can process information similar to the human brain by making associations and by consuming sparse information to solve very complex problems.

Characteristic	Omnipresent—Sense	Cognitive—Think and Learn	Autonomous—Act
What it is	Machines are able to sense like a human nerve system, which is constantly collecting, filtering, and prioritizing information.	Machines that think and learn have human-equivalent problem-solving capabilities, consciously remember their experiences, and continuously adapt.	Machines act autonomously within predefined borders: they are fully autonomous, with no human interaction or "through humans."
The key enablers	• Pervasive digitization, Internet of things, connected devices • Big data • Low cost of storage • Advanced technologies in language, gesture, and facial-expression recognition	• Artificial intelligence • Machine learning, pattern recognition • Cognitive systems	• Faster, better, cheaper, more efficient than humans • Highly automated processes • Ability to execute tasks • Goal-seeking machines
Examples in marketing	• Understand customer environment and context (e.g., weather) • Track customer behaviors • Provide knowledge (e.g., Wikipedia)	• Create psychological profiles • Predict buying behaviors • Link marketing actions to outcomes (e.g., promotions, personalization)	• Show context-sensitive promotions • Distribute machine-generated ads • Orchestrate marketing campaigns • Advise customer on phone/in app

Figure 1: Key Characteristics of Smart Machines

The Ingredients of a Smart Machine

Many characteristics distinguish traditional software applications from Smart Machines. Those are depicted in the figure below and will be explained in detail in the following chapters. An incentive and rule system needs to be set for individual Smart Machines, providing a purpose for the

Smart Machine to exist (e.g., as a self-driving car) and the rules it needs to obey (e.g., ethics, law, company procedures, and business goals).

★ Smart Machines can sense their environment and themselves, they can think and learn by themselves, and they can act autonomously.

In order for machines to see, feel, hear, smell, and taste like human beings do, all aspects of the physical world need to be translated into "digestible" data for the machines to process, reason, and act on. The rise of low-cost sensor technologies and the Internet of things, with its connected devices, enables the collection of data from the physical world without human interaction. All senses are needed to cover a customer's entire journey from inspiration to usage. The augmented senses of machines allow a broader, deeper, and more personalized customer experience. Sensed information is fed, interpreted, filtered, interlinked, and used to initiate further activities.

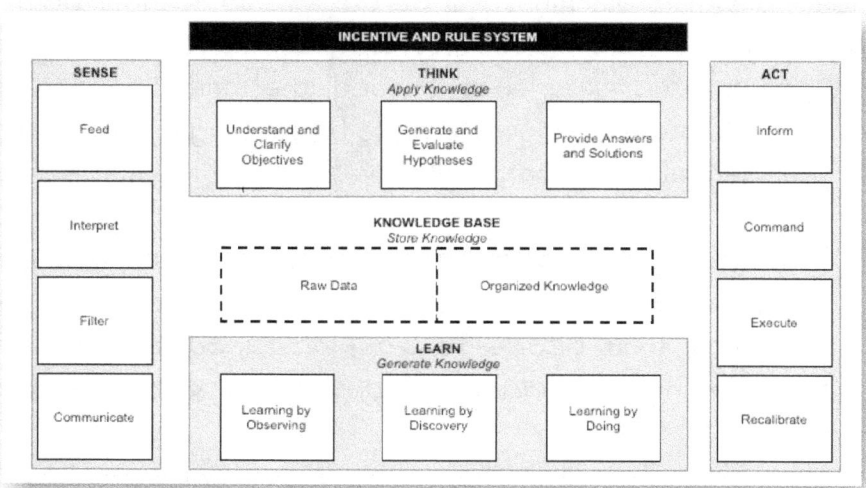

Figure 2: Components of Smart Machines

The most important ability of Smart Machines is processing the sensed information similar to the way we humans process information (i.e., empirical learning). Smart Machines are able to think and solve problems by understanding and clarifying objectives (and sometimes coming up with their own objectives), by generating and evaluating hypotheses, and by providing answers and solutions like a human would (and unlike a search machine, which simply gives a list of results). Smart Machines are self-learning; they can adapt their own algorithms through observation and discovery and by doing.

Finally, Smart Machines can act by visualizing and providing the responses to a human decision maker, by informing or even commanding a human to execute certain activities, or in the extreme case, by completely autonomously executing a business process or any other action. Based on the results of the actions, Smart Machines are able to recalibrate their goal setting.

The Impact of Smart Machines on the Marketing Profession

The impact of Smart Machines will be observable in three domains for marketing professionals. First of all, customers will get a more contextualized and personalized experience. Second, the marketing departments will be able to do more with fewer people by building on automation and scale of intelligent algorithms that take over some of the human labor.

★ Companies need to rethink their marketing mix. It is not something set universally for all customers but rather something that needs to be fine-tuned to best fit the needs of the individual customer in a given situation.

Third, there will be advances in the customer journey that are of a disruptive nature. Smart Machines will also disrupt the way we manage the four Ps of marketing—product, place, price, and promotions. *Products* will be extended to machine-driven custom design of positive customer experiences around products and services. The *place* for sales will be anywhere the customer is. The *price* can be dynamically adjusted to each individual customer in real time and dependent on context. And *promotions* will be fully automated one-to-one marketing campaigns that are optimized in real time using machine-generated content.

The marketing profession will be affected quickly and significantly by Smart Machines and the algorithmic economy. Personalizing and contextualizing the customer experience is everyone's aim. But creating meaningful continuous one-to-one interactions can only be feasible on a large scale with thousands or millions of customers if Smart Machines take over a lot of the work. This means that Smart Machines perform work that was in the past reserved for humans—for example, generating new content and supervising staff in retail stores to ensure high customer engagement. It also means that those companies that still struggle with data-driven marketing will be in deep trouble. Those who embrace Smart Machine marketing will be able to drive productivity beyond the imaginable for marketing and sales in the next decades. You cannot stop progress from happening. So it's better to focus on the new opportunities that are visible on the horizon.

Like all things in life, Smart Machines are all a matter of perspective. For marketing divisions in traditional companies, they might be seen as the biggest threat in history. Most marketing departments today rely heavily on human labor and human decision making. Shifting the work to Smart Machines will render many traditional marketing personnel redundant and will require new capabilities that the workforce does not necessarily have. For others, like Silicon Valley start-ups and companies, Smart Machines create a once-in-a-lifetime opportunity. Smart Machines allow them to scale their limited resources and thus be able to challenge even the largest established players in their own strongholds, whether that is retail, consumer goods, banking, insurance, manufacturing, entertainment, or any other type of industry that requires marketing.

Preparing for the Future of Marketing

A major question for marketing leaders will be, what are the skills and capabilities that you need to grow? Not everything is plannable today.

Nobody can predict how fast certain Smart Machine applications will achieve adoption. What we do know is that they will come and that every marketing department needs to be prepared. This book gives you a glimpse into the medium and long-term future of marketing so that you can anticipate what is needed to be successful tomorrow.

This book is for marketing managers who want to get ready for the next revolution in their profession—those who are not working in Silicon Valley, and those who are not already in the middle of breaking the next human frontier by creating yet another brilliant Smart Machine. It all starts with understanding the impending new technologies and their impact on marketing. We aim to empower those marketing managers of traditional large and medium-size companies to compete with many of the most innovative start-ups and to defend their business. It empowers them to understand the implications of Smart Machines for marketing and begin to prepare their enterprise for the disruptions that are yet to come.

This book is divided into three parts, starting with painting a picture of the future of marketing, then going into the details of how Smart Machines actually work, and finally providing some advice on how marketing managers can start their their transformation to prepare for the future.

The first part of the book, "The Future of Marketing," describes how we believe Smart Machines might transform marketing from the perspective of a marketing manager. The aim is to predict how the profession will change and how the marketing mix (product, price, place, promotion, etc.) of the future will be managed. We write about what a day in the life of a marketing manager will be like in ten years. These speculative stories are meant to stimulate the imagination, but they also take a realistic view of what we can expect when we extrapolate from the trends we see today. This section concludes with real-life examples that show some of the current developments in the area of Smart Machine marketing.

The second part of the book, "The Forces Behind," investigates the three critical capabilities of Smart Machines. Machines will become omnipresent, cognitive, and autonomous. But this will not happen overnight. Every company needs to prepare its business for those three essential capabilities and ensure that the capabilities are being used to transform all marketing activities. We show how Smart Machines use their five senses to make them omnipresent with the help of the Internet of things, wearable devices, mobiles phones, and sensors. We explain the deep learning capabilities of cognitive computing that give Smart Machines the ability to think and learn, solve complex problems in environments that have been difficult for computers in the past, and communicate with humans in natural language. And we investigate the potential to automate many of a company's day-to-day decisions and activities by letting Smart Machines act autonomously.

The third part of this book, "The Transformation Journey," focuses on explaining the implications of Smart Machines for marketing. It will help you to get your organization on track with building a business that is customer-centric with a solid marketing data foundation and strong capabilities in analytics and data science. We present case studies of successful marketing transformations and digital innovations of the last few years that can be an inspiration for starting to manage your transformation journey. And this book part gives you the steps your marketing department can take to prepare for the age of algorithmic economy and provides some advice on how to overcome the key challenges on the way: cultural resistance, social impact, cybersecurity, data protection, and digital ethics. It enables you to start your marketing transformation once you finish reading this book.

Changes will not come overnight, and there is still time to react. We hope you will enjoy reading our book and that it will provide you with new insight and provoke many further questions.

Part I

The Future of Marketing

Chapter 2

Reshaping the Four P's and Customer Interaction Across Industries

The best way to predict the future is to invent it!

—STEVE JOBS

The Way Smart Machines Change Your Marketing Mix and the Four Ps

The basic principles of marketing will still stay the same—the same but different. Smart Machines will move the frontier of what is achievable with computers. In particular, the needs and context of each individual customer can be taken much more into account to create a marketing mix that is just right for this particular customer. Add the growing fusion of the physical and digital world and the opportunities are nearly endless.

* The traditional marketing mix needs some rework with the advancement of Smart Machines. The four Ps become more individualized and digitized.

	Product	Place	Price	Promotion
Traditional Marketing	Limited, static customization options	Stores (physical, online, mobile)	Relatively static pricing, discrimination for special buyer groups (e.g., students)	Promotions by segment, optimized for each individual segment using human-generated content
Marketing with Smart Machines	Machine-driven custom design of positive customer experiences around products and services	Anywhere the customer is	Can be dynamically adjusted to each individual customer in real time and dependent on context	Fully automated one-to-one marketing campaign, optimized in real time using machine-generated content

Figure 3: Smart Machines and the Four Ps

Product: From Mass Products to Individual Experiences

In the more traditional sense, Smart Machines can assist in product development by coming up with and gathering feedback on new product ideas and features. They allow product managers to react quicker to market movements, be faster in detecting consumer trends, and monitor and manage brands, products, and portfolios. Smart Machines are able to understand buying patterns and preferences of customers and to identify if a segment would be interested in a new offering. Furthermore, they can track the recent developments in competitors' products and customers' sentiments about those products.

★ We are moving to an economy that focuses on the quality of the experiences (mainly in business to consumer, or B2C) and the effectiveness and efficiency for a customer (mainly in business to business, or B2B), which shifts the *product-dominant* logic to a *service-dominant* logic.

Even more importantly, Smart Machines are your best friend in helping you shift your business to an economy that is no longer about products but rather about experiences. Think of the Apple iPhone, which has become the best-selling device in the world, not due to its hardware and software properties, but rather through its cutting-edge customer experience and the ecosystem of apps and services that surround it. In a way, products derive their value only through usage—the service they provide. In a service-centered view of products, the focus is on the ongoing relationship with the customer rather than the actual sales transactions of the customer who buys the product. Hence, Smart Machines can enable a company to personalize and contextualize customer experiences, assess the overall quality of each individual customer's experience, and find ways to improve the customer journey, oftentimes within hours, minutes, or even seconds.

Place: From Channels to Real-Time Anywhere

One of the biggest advantages of Smart Machines is that they are available 24-7 and can support the customer wherever he or she is. Marketing managers should therefore rethink the channels they use to sell their products or services. There might be new opportunities via routes like the Internet of things, wearable devices, mobile applications, social networks, and any shoppable content outside of the traditional channels. In a real-time anywhere sales environment, it will be crucial for the Smart Machine to always have a view of the current context of the customer. This includes the state of the individual customer journey, a prediction of what the customer has on his or her mind and his or her intent, the examination of regular patterns like going to work and to the gym, and the environmental and social context, such as the local weather or local public holidays.

> ★ Gartner predicts that by the end of 2018, customer digital assistants will recognize individuals by face and voice across channels and partners.[6]

Smart Machines are also great at providing a consistent experience across channels, as they can keep track of all customer interactions, support human staff in the store or call center, and measure the effectiveness of each channel. In particular, biometrics recognition (e.g., fingerprint, face, or voice) can help to identify a customer independent of the channel that the customer uses.

Price: When Pricing Becomes Personal and Dynamic

Smart Machines can calculate the price sensitivity of each customer segment or even of each individual customer. This enables marketing managers to understand the effect and implication of a price change for a product or service. Smart Machines can then dynamically adjust the pricing in real time and dependent on context. For example, a coupon can be sent to a particular customer group or used for a specific product bundle with a special price that fits the price sensitivity of the customer in the best way.

> ★ Amazon makes price changes according to the time of the day consumers are most likely to be shopping for a particular category.

Another use for Smart Machines is updating prices according to the context of the customers—for example, the time of day, the weather, the season, local events, and many other aspects that could result in a higher profit through dynamic pricing optimization.

Promotion: The Campaign Manager Who Knows It All

A major application of Smart Machines is to attract, engage, convert, and retain customers. Advertising is gradually being generated and run with far more automation boosted by self-learning algorithms and real-time measurement. Today Smart Machines are already used for programmatic buying, which is any ad buy that gets processed through machines. The most prominent example is buying ads through computer-run auctions—known as *real-time bidding*. It will gradually expand to more traditional media (e.g., radio, print, and TV). Smart Machines can put together modular elements to create individual messages and lead consumers through the marketing funnel in a straightforward manner. In the future, Smart Machines will orchestrate programmatic marketing campaigns across all channels nearly autonomously.

★ According to Gartner, by 2018, 20 percent of all business content will be authored by machines.[7]

Furthermore, Smart Machines can personalize and contextualize promotions and gather feedback on the success of these promotions to continuously improve their algorithms. They can even generate personalized content by reconfiguring text components, putting together the most relevant news, or writing microstories or longer texts all by themselves.

★ Smart Machines can continuously learn even in runtime mode to improve their algorithms that send out promotions and optimize customer lifetime value.

In the extreme case, Smart Machines can manage all communications with the customer and identify and create new sales leads. They can predict customers' propensity to buy and can improve their predictions as they observe the results and attribute sales to the channels and promotions that have been significant. In this way, Smart Machines can continuously optimize the media mix. Based on customer sentiments on social media and the Internet, the contribution and harm caused to the brand by the promotions can be monitored and improved.

How Smart Machines Contextualize and Personalize Customer Interactions

The rules of engagement are being realigned... Advertising is getting a new operating system.[8]

—*DIFFFERENT STRATEGIEAGENTUR*

With the help of Smart Machines, marketing managers can contextualize and personalize all the interactions with their customers. *Contextualization* involves taking the current, past, and future context of the customer into account with regard to time, place, and situation. The context of the marketing message can be chosen depending on where the customer is and what he or she does. An advertisement for a restaurant might work best when the customer feels hungry on the way home from work and is looking for good places to eat on the way. Depending on where the customer is, there are other local options to explore. Other aspects of the context might also determine the situation the customer is in, which has an impact on marketing messages. If you know, for example, that it is supposed to rain all day in the city where the customer lives, you can advise your customer to use a different mode of transportation rather than his or her bicycle.

Type of Contextualization	Example
Time	"You're on your way home. Are you looking for a great place to eat?"
Place	"There are local events in the area you might be interested in."
Situation	"The weather outside is frightful tonight; you should not take the bike."

Table 1: Types of Contextualization

Personalization requires understanding the specific characteristics of the customer. You can adapt the style of your marketing messages to your individual customer. For instance, your customer might be a fact-driven person and expect you to give him or her just the facts. A Smart Machine can likewise learn the preferred marketing and sales channel. A marketeer might find out that young couples who plan to buy a house prefer personal interaction when it comes to choosing the right provider for their mortgage. The content of the marketing message can be chosen to better fit the circumstances of the individual customer: for example, by not trying to sell meat to a vegetarian.

Type of Personalization	Example
Communication Style	"We know you are a fact-driven person, so we will just give you the facts."
Communication Channel	"We understand that you prefer personal interaction when it comes to your mortgage."
Message Content	"You told us that you are a vegetarian. Here are some food recommendations."
Service Offerings	"We think that you like action movies with Sylvester Stallone—no-nonsense kinds of films."
Product Offerings	"We know that you often take photos, why don't you get a smartphone with a zoom objective extension?"

Table 2: Types of Personalization

Services and products can be personalized too. In the good old days many, many years ago, a personalized service would look like this: you come into the bakery, and the baker says, "I noticed that every Wednesday you buy four pretzels. We were about to run out, so I set some aside for you."

Today, personalized service is given to millions using customer data analytics. For example, media-streaming service provider Netflix knows that you like action movies with Sylvester Stallone and maybe some with Bruce Willis, but certainly no romantic nonsense like *Titanic* or *Shakespeare in Love.* Personalizing the product in the olden-days bakery might involve a baker saying, "Last time you told me that you like bread with sesame sprinkles. I made some especially for you!" Today, it might be your own car that suggests the restaurant that would be best for you to try out next.

Personalization and contextualization are certainly some of the most impact areas of Smart Machines. Other impact areas will differ by industry. The next section looks at trends and implications of Smart Machines that are more industry specific.

Applications of Smart Machine Marketing, Industry by Industry

How quickly Smart Machines will transform marketing depends on the industry, as the speed of adoption differs by industry. Just as digital transformation in past years has been led by consumer-driven industries like retail, consumer goods, and media, we can expect a similar development for Smart Machines. In the following section, we give an overview of some of the leading developments in each industry sector.

* Applications of Smart Machines can differ from industry to industry. You need to find the sweet spots and the strategic differentiators for your business.

The following use cases should provide an inspirational entry point to the art of the possible in each respective industry.

Retail: The Personal Shopping Adviser 24-7

One of the early adoptions of Smart Machines has been by virtual shopping advisers. Retailers are experimenting with intelligent machines that guide the customer through the inspiration and buying process. We also see the first concierge robots being put to work at shops and hotels. Those shopping advisers or concierge robots will be able to help navigate the client through every interaction, independent of channel. Machines will recognize the customer and continue the interaction from the last point of contact. This allows more personalized and targeted engagement based on customer status (e.g., VIP customer, loyal customer, or first-time customer) and phase in the customer journey (awareness-focused versus transaction-focused interaction). Given the cognitive capabilities of voice and face recognition, robots can modify the way they speak or respond based on the real-time sentiment and mood (e.g., happy, excited, or stressed). Moreover, cross- and upselling will also be lifted to a whole new level if Smart Machines leverage big data and algorithms to inspire customers with gift ideas or fashion combinations.

Some of these interactions will be fully and autonomously performed by Smart Machines. In more complex selling situations, Smart Machines will help humans by offering real-time insight and advice to close the sale. Competitive advantage will move from human selling skills to machine-augmented overall selling capabilities. Therefore, the companies that are able to incorporate learnings from their best sellers or experiences into algorithm- and machine-driven interaction are most likely to outperform their competitors. However, we also believe that physical experiences will remain a source of differentiation in a fully connected world, as they speak to our pure human senses in the realms of tasting, smelling, touching, hearing, and seeing.

Media and Entertainment: The Personal Reputation Coach

In a world full of digital and physical noise, it is important to be relevant to the right people and to have the right message. Smart Machines will not only help media companies understand, collect, and curate content, but they will also help to shape the message companies and professionals want to convey to the right audience—even the right sentiment in that moment of media consumption.

Imagine the power of a personal reputation coach who helps you to develop your brand and identity based on your personal values. Smart Machines will combine structured as well as unstructured content (i.e., text and audio) in real time to understand how messages will be perceived, evaluated, or put into context by journalists, blogs, social media gurus, and competitors. They can also help you understand the reach and impact of the individual media post, which helps to filter out the noise from the relevant content. Your personal reputation coach will then help you to shape the response and automatically create a tone for the message. This will have a tremendous impact on the whole PR and communication industry, as much of the brand and reputation assessment can be fully automated. The content creation and curation will also have a high degree of automation because machines will be able to compile messages and curate predefined content.

The content explosion around digital media and its importance in driving customer interest, attention, and engagement will require every company to become more of a media company. Smart Machines can help navigate through the complexities and challenges of finding and curating meaningful content for every customer interaction. As Smart Machines are also becoming more creative, human creativity will still have the competitive edge for the near future.

Transportation and Logistics: Autonomous Delivery

We have seen many improvements through big data in logistic networks planning and route management. Now Smart Machines are helping warehouse staff to speed up and improve the pick-and-pack process by projecting instructions on a screen—for example, on Google Glass. This is only a first step into more autonomous delivery. For the near future, humans remain the key source for fulfilling some of the activities in the delivery chain, as physical movements are still very expensive if performed by machines. As more and more devices, cars, warehouses, inventories, and orders are connected, the more opportunities there will be for Smart Machines to optimize the value chain through parameters like weather, traffic, delivery windows (based on availability of customer), and utilization (i.e., staff and trucks). The opportunity for marketing lies in the integration of all relevant information into the four Ps, allowing more real-time flexibility on personalized offers and special campaigns. Combined with predictive models, this will increase the percentage of build-to-order and stock-to-order models and help drive down costs of warehouse space and transportation modes.

With more and more things being connected through the "Internet of things," the more Smart Machines are needed to understand, structure, and process the flow of data and information in a hyperconnected world. Companies should look for efficiency gains not only in driving down cost, but also in how to build new business around the additional insight.

In the personal transport industry, there will be a major shift with self-driving cars. Fewer consumers will own their own cars. Instead they will rely on providers of multimodal mobility services that book the whole journey with a few clicks, combining flights, self-driving car services, and public transportation. Companies like Uber will most likely be winners of these trends.

Financial Services: War on Problem Solving!

Do you remember how when you wanted to buy a car, you needed to speak to your bank to get the loan? Later, car companies not only sold the car but also helped you finance it directly and maybe even offered you insurance. Now, with the shared economy, ownership is no longer the ultimate source of satisfaction for customers. They want flexible pay-as-you-go models that are priced on miles, usage, time, etc.

Financial institutions now can use Smart Machines to help combine their offerings in front of the customer in real time. In the case of providing mobility services, Smart Machines could help calculate the premium the customer has to pay given the specific parameters (customer profile, model of use, etc.), package it for the reseller or service provider, and integrate it into the financial supply chain of the bank. Such vertical services allow fast adoption to new markets or businesses while connecting dynamic customer demand with solid financial planning and risk considerations. The battle, however, is over who will be orchestrating this in the future and who will get the profitable part of the business, which is "solutioning" toward the customer.

Manufacturing: Fully Automated Supply Chain

Today we are already seeing fully automated production sites and connected supply chains. Many production processes are being performed by machines and only controlled by humans. Smart Machines will drive further automation by extremely streamlining or eliminating those pure controlling and surveillance processes. This will not only eliminate human controls but also improve the quality and effectiveness of any controls, as Smart Machines can sense and analyze production processes and sites independent of time of day, lack of motivation, and location. They will also learn much faster and adapt by improving their algorithms based on the massive amount of sensed data (e.g., images and machine noises). This will require a different skill set for factory workers, who will need more understanding of the data insight rather than the pure production process only.

Besides further automation, Smart Machines will lead the Industry 4.0 transformation, which is all about the connection of smart factories, connected devices (Internet of things), and connected services (Internet of services).[9] Smart Machines will help to assess and predict productivity gains, quality improvements, and speed of adoption on customer demands based on internal data (e.g., suppliers and connected factories), customer data (e.g., order backlog and customer feedback and satisfaction), and external data (e.g., weather data). We will probably see a new type of original design manufacturer (ODM) that will produce a much wider range of products for many more brands as they switch and adjust their machinery in near real time, allowing fast build-to-order production processes. Just-in-time maintenance based on peer-to-peer real time and historic component health data is another example where Smart Machines will drive less downtime and therefore increase production productivity. Future competitive advantages will largely come from the capability of a manufacturer to increase the "cleverness" and intelligence of its Smart Machines.

How Does This All Relate to Your Job and Company?

Our industry examples offer just a small fragment of what will be possible with Smart Machines. Why don't you take a moment to think about the possibilities and opportunities for applying Smart Machine in your company, industry, customer interaction, and internal collaboration? In the next chapter, in order to support your imagination, we relate the art of the possible to the everyday life of a marketing manager in the future. If there is one thing certain about the future, it is that our professional lives will change. How exactly they will change can be only speculation. Let's have a try!

Chapter 3

. . .

A Day in the Life of a Marketing Manager in Ten Years

All cartoon characters and fables must be exaggeration, caricatures. It is the very nature of fantasy and fable.

—WALT DISNEY

The dream factory of Hollywood constantly gives us a window to the future. Human imagination and creativity have driven the boundaries of the art of the possible to new, exciting developments that the previous generation couldn't even think of. In contrast, many of us don't think about how our working life will look in the coming years. Still, most of the workforce is reacting to trends by adopting new methods and technologies rather than actively redefining the way of working. Honestly speaking, we do not believe in some things until they hit us in the face. This is just human nature. To inspire the imagination of the readers of this book, we've created a fictional day in the life of a marketing manager in the future.

8:00 a.m. Morning Briefing: Meet the Smart Machine Adviser

The marketing VP is getting ready for the daily morning briefing with his Smart Machine adviser (SMA). It will be a lively discussion today, as a competitor is attacking the company's blockbuster product. The VP has been blindsided, and the SMA is under pressure to explain why it missed this development.

Marketing VP: How big is the impact on our revenue and profit?

SMA: Given the market position of the competitor, the past product launches, and the market reach, I see a seventy percent probability that this competing product will conquer ten percent of our market share and will erode our profit margin by five percent globally and fifteen percent in the United States.

Marketing VP: Seventy percent is still a high margin of error. SMA, what is the first indication of the consumers?

SMA: Ninety percent of early buyers responded enthusiastically on the price and ease of use. Thirty percent don't like the design but think it is a good bargain.

Marketing VP: Do we already have a view from our product team?

SMA: The product team does not think the competitor can match our design. Based on the early analysis, I only agree fifty percent with that statement.

Marketing VP: This is a critical situation. Please execute routine "urgent competitor threat" and prepare the respective managers for an urgent virtual meeting in thirty minutes!

This conversation will happen in almost every marketing organization in the future and illustrates some of the key future imperatives.

First, marketing organizations will be able to get real-time intelligence on the four Ps. The data collection, preparation, analytics, and reporting process will be fully automated. However, the constant improvement process will, along with machine recommendation, also require humans to improve algorithms, develop new data models, and of course integrate new sources of information through application program interfaces (APIs).

Second, the instant feedback from customers, buyers, and experts will drive immediate actions, which will be executed either fully autonomously (through machines or humans) or semiautonomously (where marketing staff will take over most of the response based on alternate suggestions).

Third, because 100 percent probability and predictability will still be an illusion, human strategic choices, entrepreneurial risk, and creative ideas will make the difference in competitive advantage. However, the capability within an organization for improving and innovating their Smart Machines will be equally important.

10:00 a.m. Deep Insight: Who Is Your Audience? Now!

The marketing VP is meeting with his core management team, which consists of the creative director, the experience manager, the head of algorithms, and the offering and solutions leader.

Marketing VP: Gentlemen, we are under attack. I'm sure you have received the briefing from the SMA. This is a severe situation that requires immediate counteraction. Based on our first insight, we need to target those customers with the highest propensity to be attracted by the new product. Any suggestions?

Experience Manager: Let's start by defining the persona using our fifteen-minute power sprint approach to better understand how to set up countermeasures.

Head of Algorithms: Let's be as specific as possible, as it will help the SMA to work with the right audiences.

After a very intensive power sprint, the team defines "Jason Cheap" as the persona and uploads the description into the "Campaign and Audience Now" dashboard. Given the live environment (Monday at 10:00 a.m. in March), the dashboard shows the live audience reach based on the persona. It also shows the paid and earned media reach, and the spend indication of the competitor. As the probability indication in the morning meeting was only about 70 percent, the marketing VP and the team need to test and learn to better understand how they can convince their current or potential customers to go with their product. After thirty minutes in the live campaign, it looks like only one very specific audience is attracted to the competitive product and can only be convinced with special offers or significant paid spend.

> **Marketing VP:** Not as bad as I thought. Well, I hope we did not miss anything this time. Let's disengage from this respective customer group and focus the spend on our high-value prospects.

The whole team feels relieved after the live campaign, as it appears that the competitive product is not dangerous to the core business.

Companies today understand that they need to start from the customer, buyer, or user to create meaningful experiences. Books, trainings, and methods around design thinking have flooded the economy and are a strong signal that it has become mainstream. On the other hand, companies fall short in predicting the success of marketing campaigns or assets for a given target audience. While prediction models based on advanced data insight will improve prediction quality, the real change comes through real-time feedback from the audience based on cognitive machine-learning capabilities.

Humans will still be the source for creativity and inspiration on how to engage with their audience. Machines will help increase the impact and responsiveness by providing recommendations on the best way to engage (device, platform, time of the day, content, etc.) and real-time feedback on the "live" audience. It is still human creativity and imagination that create a competitive advantage. However, creativity will be needed not only for the classic marketing assets but also for the data models, algorithms, and combination of technologies.

1:00 p.m. Content Curation: Is Our Creative Idea Working?

The creative director is discussing with the Smart Machine the success of the newest creative idea, which is especially focused on relaxed passengers in planes, trains, and cars.

Creative Director: What are the numbers telling us, SMA? Are we getting the results we expected?

SMA: We achieve an average conversion rate of twenty-two percent. This is in our expected range of twenty to twenty-five percent. Only the conversation rate for car passengers is significantly below average at ten percent.

Creative Director: Can you analyze which situation the car passengers are engaged in?

SMA: Eighty-five percent of the passengers have clicked while the car was going over fifty-five miles per hour and were traveling for more than one hour. Seems we reach our audience on longer-distance travel, mainly on the highway.

Creative Director: OK! Please adjust the targeting accordingly.

In ten years most of the customer touch points will be digitized. Connected cars, smart devices, digital billboards, IPTV, digital radio, and many more will enable a highly programmatic and personalized engagement with the customer. Moreover, marketers can take greater creative risk in producing exciting, relevant, and helpful content.

Content will be curated based on multiple external and internal content sources. Based on the personal preferences of look-alike audiences, content curation will happen in milliseconds in front of the customer and will be presented in an appealing way. This requires content produced and stored in small content pieces such as text, video or image, and audio. Marketers need to understand how to tell the same story with many different options. Machines will help to access the feedback loop and learn as they go; however, producing creative content will still be a predominant domain of humans.

3:00 p.m. Building New Marketing Assets: My Personal Front End!

Branded content, content marketing, and digital marketing assets infused with cognitive technologies will change the way we do marketing in the future. The marketing VP and creative director are discussing how they can drive more excitement around their brand.

Marketing VP: I received the message on our effectiveness in engaging car passengers. Right now we are only reaching high engagement figures with the long-distance travelers. Any idea on how we can also engage the short-distance travelers or commuters?

Creative Director: Let's do some ideation. SMA, what are the leading parameters for engaging this kind of audience?

SMA: Sixty-five percent expect meaningful content that helps them to prepare for work. Thirty percent want light entertainment where they can drift off. Five percent want no entertainment at all.

Marketing VP: Let's think about a joined campaign with one of the car manufacturers. What do you think?

Creative Director: "Your personalized infotainment delivered with your favorite look and feel into your car."

Marketing VP: Sounds great. Please work with SMA on finding the right partner and at least five alternative styles for the target audience, and see if we can monetize or cofund the campaign with some of our publishers.

Imagine how companies can use marketing budgets to create useful digital media assets and apps for the customer. Marketing, sales, and service will eventually merge into one customer engagement practice. In the eyes of the customer, every interaction is valuable, and every interaction counts. Companies will build in-car apps that will not only show relevant content as news or location-based offers but will also allow customers to get the look and feel they are used to from their favorite design and brands. Smart Machines will help to adapt to different user scenarios and will show a different selection of marketing or usage-relevant media assets based on the user mode. For in-car experience, this means the distinction between self-driving, autonomous driving, and purpose of driving (work, leisure, etc.) Humans will define the experience, and machines will create the experience and curate the content and assets.

5:00 p.m. Marketing Measurements: Do They Still Matter?

The experience manager is assessing the patterns that lead to a long-term customer relationship.

> **Experience Manager:** What makes a happy customer for us, SMA?
> **SMA:** Please specify what you mean by "happy customer."
> **Experience Manager:** A customer who gives us high customer satisfaction ratings, writes positively about our products, and is loyal over a longer period of time or is just buying from us on a regular basis.
> **SMA:** When it comes to revenue and profitability, our most profitable clients are buying at least two products per year, are buying at least one product as a gift every two years, and are writing five reviews per year, and seventy percent have a relationship with us that is longer than seven years.
> **Experience Manager:** Do we know what they like the most about our products?

SMA: Ninety-five percent see our quality as superior to comparable products in the market. Only forty percent buy because they also like the design. This number has been going down from sixty percent two years ago. Eighty-five percent say it is easy to get in contact with us independent of channel. Ninety percent like our physical store and partner network, where they can pop in at any time.
Experience Manager: We have been investing heavily in our physical network. Please analyze for tomorrow's meeting the cost per customer for our owned channels and partner channels.

If measurements can be calculated and reported in real time, how relevant are they given the key performance indicator (KPI) mantra of today's world? We believe they still will be important, as they help humans and machines understand the success of previous actions, audience preferences, and competitive advantages. However, measurements will be much more flexible in the way you utilize different indicators to drive behavior in your company, for your business partners, and for customers. Every company will be able to calculate most of today's standard KPIs, but not all will be able to combine different KPIs and operational performance indicators (OPIs) to new scorecards or KPI measures. The better companies understand the interdependency of KPIs and measures through machine learning and discovery, the better they can influence behavior and drive machine as well as human actions.

7:00 p.m. Being Innovative: Should I Network with Humans or Machines?

The marketing VP is leaving the office to attend the yearly marketing summit. He will not be alone, as the SMA is attending as well.

Marketing VP: SMA, tonight I want to introduce you to some of the thought leaders of the future of marketing. Our key focus is to validate our three-year strategy with the projections and studies done by leading marketing university professors.

SMA: Do you have any special part of the strategy in mind?

Marketing VP: Yes, I'm especially interested to know if our new engagement platform is able to engage in the way our customers and prospects will search and look for products in that given time of the road map.

After the keynote session, the marketing VP is having a face-to-face meeting with the keynote speaker, Dr. Future.

Marketing VP: Thanks, Dr. Future, for the inspiring ideas on the next evolution of marketing. Is it OK that my Smart Machine Adviser is attending the session?

Dr. Future: Of course. My Smart Research Machine (SRM) is also attending, in case you want to go deeper into some of our findings.

Marketing VP: Yes, definitely. I would to validate our road map for the customer engagement platform with your projection of personal communication styles and technologies over the next three years. SMA, can you please present the key road-map components, including our hypotheses around the parameters?

SMA: Dr. Future, Smart Research Machine, our road map consists of five steps, which I will outline in detail. If you have any questions, please jump in. Is there any specific information you need to better match to your research?

Dr. Future: Smart Research Machine, I think we need the key input factors by confidence interval and priority, don't we?

SRM: Yes, and your key hypotheses that you used to make the next-step conclusion.

SMA: OK, SRM, I just sent you all the key data we used to formulate the hypotheses. Dr. Future, I will focus on the key areas, but SRM can add details based on the data submitted if needed.

Sounds a bit strange, right? You may be asking, "How can I network with a machine, or how do machines network today?" Well, the growth of machine-to-machine communication is significantly outpacing machine-to-human interaction. Many devices speak to one another to improve room climate, driving safety, and many other things. But most of those actions are based on predefined models, and machine learning has just started to take off in that space. Google has shown with its self-studying robots example that connected machines can not only learn from their own actions but can also incorporate learnings from other machines. This will not only reduce the time to train newly built robots but also the time for upskilling and setting up new working areas.

Therefore, the more Chief Marketing Officers (CMOs) can connect with Smart Machines from vendors, partners, and other external specialists (e.g., weather data providers), the more they can increase the exposure to new data and learnings for their own machines. More data, more possible patterns, and more ways to look at the same thing will drive better decisions. But can machines connect and network on their own? We believe at some point in the future, yes, they will, but not in ten years. This may be a big relief for many CMOs, as they can continue to enjoy personal networking events, dinner meetings, and fun off-site events in the future.

Bringing It Back to Earth

In reality, some of the described situations might be further away than others. We know that many of these stories might never actually become true, since we are aware that it is impossible to predict the future. So let's get back to the facts. The next chapter gives an overview on how companies are already applying some of the new technologies and capabilities of Smart Machines today. They are not as advanced as in our previous, more speculative examples, but they clearly show that there are visible developments toward an algorithmic world of Smart Machines.

Chapter 4

Real-Life Examples of Smart Machine Marketing Today

The real enemies of our life are the "oughts" and the "ifs." They pull us backward into the unalterable past and forward into the unpredictable future. But real life takes place in the here and now.

—Henri Nouwen

Meet Amelia, Your New Smart Digital Assistant

Let's get back to some examples of what is already possible today. One of the most exciting existing use cases for Smart Machines in marketing is digital assistants. Digital assistants are Smart Machines that emulate the behavior of human assistants to serve the clients and are available 24-7. Some of them are so smart that it is hard to see much difference between them and real human assistants. A brilliant example is Amelia, a cognitive customer assistant provided by the company IPsoft.

Amelia appears on screen as an avatar, allowing customers to interact with her in natural language via a chat window. In the future she will also be able to leverage third-party voice-recognition technologies in order to allow customers to speak to her. She understands words in many languages, but in order to communicate like a native speaker, she needs the appropriate natural language parser to be integrated. She will be available in Japanese and a number of other languages this year.

Just like any new employee, Amelia needs to be trained to understand the vocabulary of a particular business domain and the process being used by the company where she is working. Typically Amelia will learn by reading handbooks that contain the relevant information, uploading process flows and reading the chat records of her colleagues. The models that Amelia creates as a result of this input are sent to a subject matter expert in order to verify or correct what has been presented. Only then is Amelia permitted to use it in real life.

If she does not know something, she will refer the query to a more experienced agent. When Amelia's human colleague joins the conversation, he can read the full script and then respond. Importantly, Amelia stays in the conversation and observes everything that is said. This way she learns how to resolve that query independently in future. When there is no one else to escalate to immediately, Amelia will let the customer know that he will be contacted with an answer the next day. Amelia is a superfast learner. In beta trials with one enterprise partner, Amelia handled fewer than 10 percent of all incoming calls during the first week, but by the end of the first month, that number had jumped to 42 percent, and by the close of month number two, Amelia was successfully handling 61 percent of incoming requests.

Amelia continues to learn as she works. Her *neural ontology* stores knowledge of the information that is required in order to fulfill her role. The semantic memory and network she builds here allow her to understand the concepts conveyed in the information and relationships between those concepts. Her *process ontology* describes the steps in a process that need to be followed, in particular when using other administrative IT systems to execute a process flow. Her *episodic memory* stores the experience of all the interactions that have taken place in the past and speeds up her ability to recognize how to best fulfill the customer's goal. And finally, her *emotional ontology* maps out the emotional state of the customer she is interacting with and allows her to respond appropriately, just as a human would. Amelia draws on all these capabilities in order to best understand what the customer's intent is and how to respond to this request most efficiently. For example, if a customer were to contact Amelia because he had lost his luggage, Amelia would remain focused on how to resolve this and not be distracted from her task even if the customer, who was getting anxious about it getting late, asked an unrelated but totally natural question such as "What is the time?"

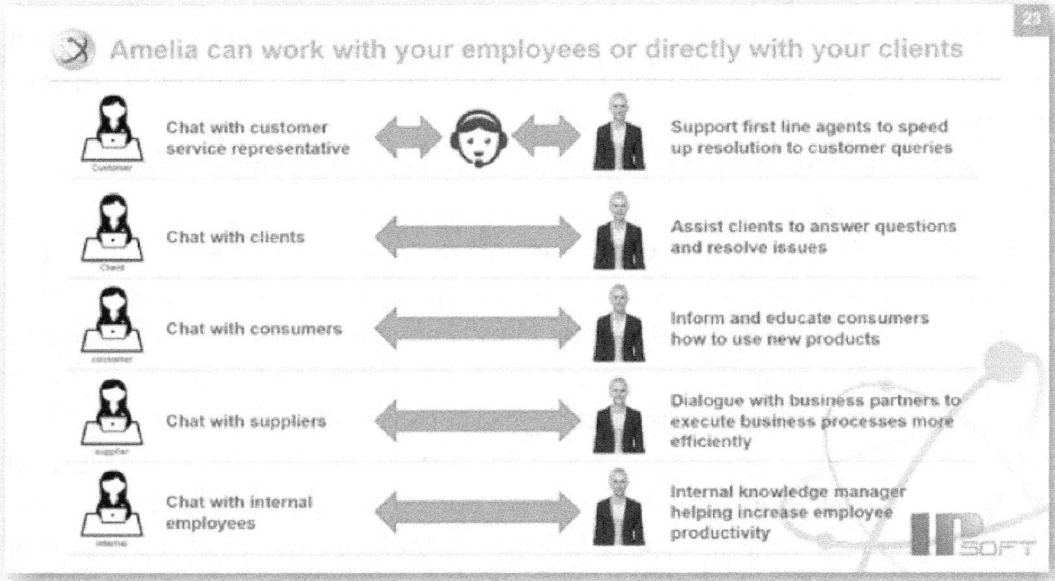

Figure 4: Use Cases for Amelia

How Amelia Builds Her Domain-Specific Neural Ontology

When Amelia reads a large block of text, she absorbs all the domain information contained by understanding the concepts included in the passage. Amelia starts building a semantic network of all these concepts and how they relate to one another. When there are conflicting or ambiguous points of information, Amelia highlights the need for clarification, which can be provided by domain experts. Amelia leverages research from various scholars within academia in order to understand natural language.

In particular, she uses the "universal parser" from Stanford University to understand grammar and the definition of common words.

Interestingly, experience shows that in many situations, as few as ten questions make up 80 percent of the volume of inquiries received within call centers. As a result, training Amelia to be productive and have a significant impact on operations is simpler than one might think.

Amelia does not need to start with a huge amount of information. She actually builds her neural ontology as she is given new facts. Here are two real conversations we had with Amelia during a demo.

Transcript One:

> **User:** All birds can fly.
> **User:** All penguins are birds.
> **User:** Can penguins fly?
> **Amelia:** Yes.
> **User:** All penguins cannot fly.
> **Amelia:** I am sorry to hear.
> **User:** Can penguins fly?
> **Amelia:** No.
> **User:** Can birds fly?
> **Amelia:** Yes.

Transcript Two:

> **User:** All personal information is processed in accordance with the Dutch Personal Protection Act.
> **User:** Passengers shall provide the carrier with their personal information to make a reservation.
> **User:** Do you process my personal information?
> **Amelia:** Yes.
> **User:** Who has to provide personal information?
> **Amelia:** Passengers.

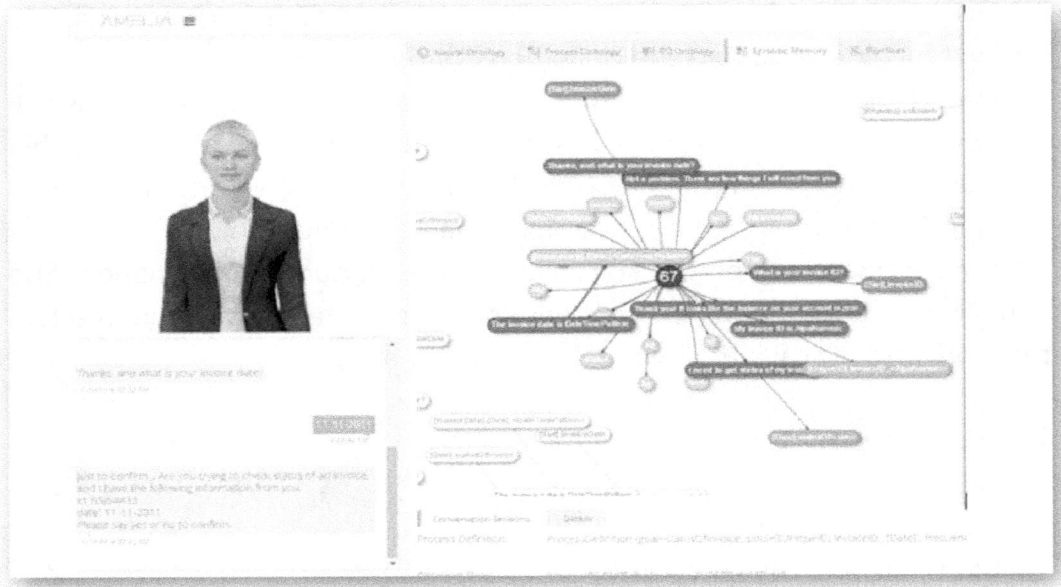

Figure 5: Neural Ontology of Amelia

Process Ontology for Understanding Questions

Just like a human agent, Amelia can connect to many other systems in order to execute tasks. For example, she can access common back-end administrative management platforms such as HR systems, a ticketing system, and a flight passenger system. She simply has to be trained when to invoke certain steps by building a process ontology. Just like any other employee, Amelia needs to be authorized to access those other systems. Similarly, she will check on the authorization levels of the customer she is serving. For instance, she might need to authenticate someone's identify before carrying out a specific action. If for any reason the customer provides strange answers, Amelia will escalate to a human operator.

For instance, in this scenario Amelia is working at an airline, helping deal with lost luggage queries. The business value of her work is measured in customer satisfaction scores. Take the case of a customer who flies from Moscow to London and is searching for his luggage. Instead of waiting in a line for hours to report the issue, Amelia could provide immediate 24-7 advice on what is being done to resolve the issue.

Here is another example transcript from a live demo. This one applies a process ontology as part of the airline example.

Transcript Three:

User: Can you help me find my luggage?
Amelia: Do you have the tag number?
User: I can't find it.
Amelia: Look at the left corner of your ticket.
User: Oh, here it is.
Amelia: I will now search for your luggage.
Amelia: Your luggage is available at the service desk in the main hall at Schiphol Airport.

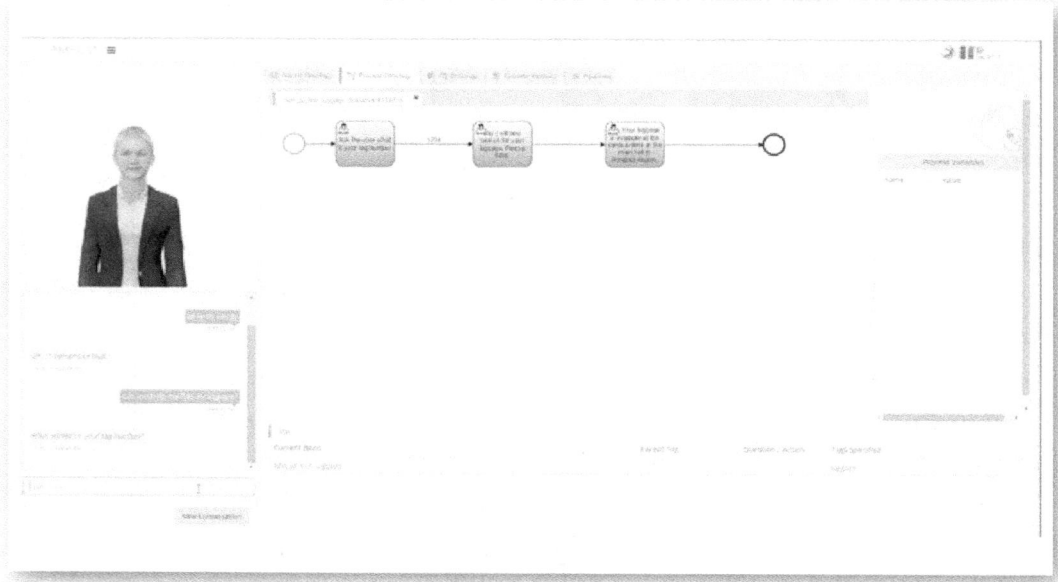

Figure 6: Process Ontology of Amelia

Episodic Memory for Remembering Past Experiences

The episodic memory saves the time sequence of events that happened in the past. Amelia reads previous chat logs between agents and customers to learn quickly how she can help customers. Often such logs are available within companies in order to monitor quality, as well as well as for training purposes. A demo set of conversations is given to Amelia covering questions from suppliers about invoice payment queries. Here is another example script from a real conversation, this time applying episodic memory.

Transcript Four:

> **User:** What is my invoice status?
> *Amelia selects the best match based on past questions and understands which questions she needs to ask. A unique ID and a date are needed from the user. There is no process flow. Algorithms are applied to hit the best response.*
> **Amelia:** Just to confirm…are you trying to check the status of an invoice with the ID?

EQ Ontology for Interpreting Emotions

Finally, Amelia is able to detect human emotions, such as whether a customer is becoming angry and frustrated or whether he is happy and enthusiastic. Her reading of the customer's emotions is based on the words used in the chat, and these are interpreted using a standard psychological model (PAD). In real time Amelia displays a customer satisfaction score that has been calculated on the conversation so far. When Amelia recognizes that someone is complaining, she can be taught to avoid selling a new product at this time.

Transcript Five:

> **User:** Amelia, I love you.
> **Amelia:** I appreciate it.
> *Customer satisfaction score goes up.*

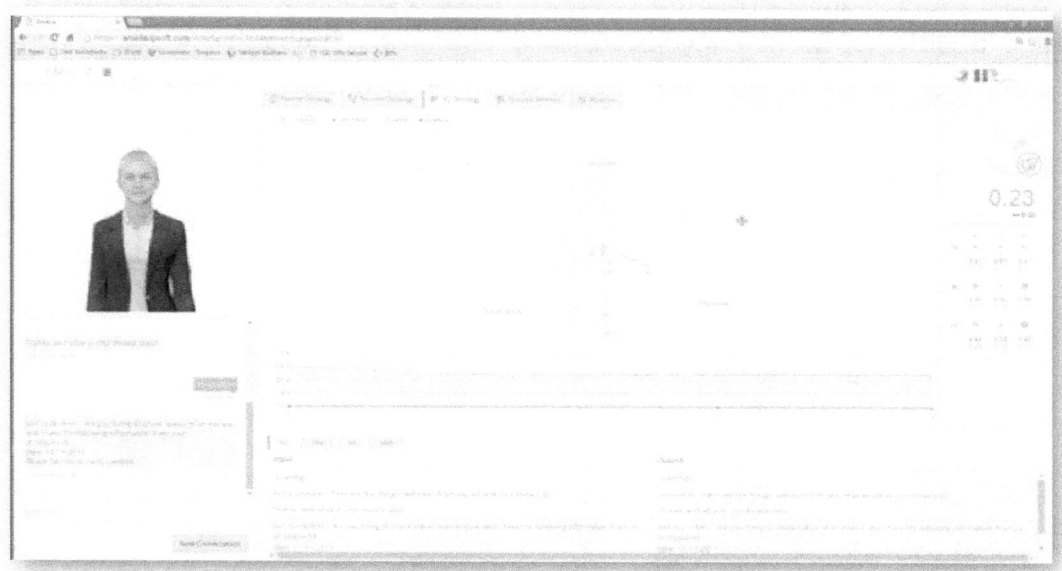

Figure 7: EQ of Amelia

The Success Story of IBM Watson—from Game Champion to Medical Doctor and Kitchen Chef

I for one welcome our new computer overlords.

—Ken Jennings, all-time Jeopardy! champion
(after the lost match against IBM Watson)

The Rules behind Jeopardy!

Most people first heard about IBM's Watson computer when it beat the two all-time champions of the American quiz game *Jeopardy!* after a three-night marathon. The game is particularly difficult for computers, since it requires understanding of very complex questions that contain puns and word plays. Watson was fed over one million pages of Wikipedia articles and a wide range of encyclopedias, dictionaries, thesauri, newswire articles, and literary works. The system was able to understand the questions posed by the moderator, search matching answers in milliseconds, and be faster at the buzzer than its human contenders.

The following examples give an overview of the sort of questions and answers in the show:[10]

Category: General Science
Clue: When hit by electrons, a phosphor gives off electromagnetic energy in this form.
Answer: Light (or Photons)

Category: Lincoln Blogs
Clue: Secretary Chase just submitted this to me for the third time; guess what, pal? This time I'm accepting it.
Answer: His resignation

Category: Head North
Clue: They're the two states you could be reentering if you're crossing Florida's northern border.
Answer: Georgia and Alabama

The victory made a huge public mark, as it demonstrated that a computing system is capable of defeating great human minds in a complex question-and-answer competition.

How IBM Watson Works

Watson is a question-answering machine capable of answering questions posed in natural language.[11] It can be fed with tons of documents to learn about a particular domain. Watson understands natural language and human communication. It generates and evaluates evidence-based hypotheses. And it learns and adapts from user selections and responses. The process for Watson when it is asked a question is as follows:

* First Watson decomposes the question, makes associations with its knowledge base, and interprets the question. A variety of search techniques is used to find the information in the knowledge base in order to create the hypothesis, including the use of multiple text search engines with different underlying approaches. The search results are soft filtered (using the likelihood of the candidate answer) to narrow down the results to a set of possible answers and evidence collected from its knowledge base, which are formulated as hypotheses.
* The evidence is then analyzed for each hypothesis in the knowledge base, and the confidence in the support for each hypothesis is calculated to create a score. Scores from equivalent answers are combined.
* Finally, one or more responses are delivered back, including a confidence level and the evidence that led to the confidence to provide transparency to the user. If the right level of confidence is not achieved, Watson can iterate and search for further answer candidates in its knowledge base to generate and test further hypotheses. Based on the feedback of responses, Watson uses machine learning to improve the answer quality, which leads to higher confidence levels.

In a nutshell, Watson is able to understand the questions posed in natural language, search for possible answers in the vast amount of data, calculate the confidence level by combining multiple factors, and provide the possible answers with the highest confidence levels.

IBM Watson as Your New Trusted Doctor

It took IBM a couple of more years to get Watson to work. One of the first application fields for Watson was to better understand the courses of diseases, symptoms, and treatments. IBM CEO Ginni Rometty called it IBM's "moonshot" in health care. She might be right, given the impact this could have on treating and curing most diseases. And the more data Watson can scan through, the better and more precise the diagnosis gets, especially for very rare diseases.

Doctor Watson's success depends heavily on the data it can digest. IBM has made significant efforts to create a database with partners that allows Watson to use the description of symptoms given to him and run through a vast amount of clinical studies, patient records, medical journals, and textbooks to list potential diseases. Moreover, Watson's machine-learning capabilities support new connections and learnings from every patient interaction. Imagine the exponential growth and additional insight as we see more and more patient interactions done with Smart Machines.

The following example provides some insight into how Watson works in identifying diseases.

First, Watson reads through a patient case description and extracts the most significant facts. This also highlights the importance of detailed case descriptions, as they help Watson to be more precise on the symptoms, which leads to a better match of the disease. Second, Watson makes a first connection of symptoms to diseases using its large database. Third, Watson collects and provides evidence to the disease connection and lists the evidence based on the most likely ones. At this point in the process, the doctor can verify or refute the evidences provided by Watson. This is crucial in order for Watson to learn and improve the diagnosis quality.

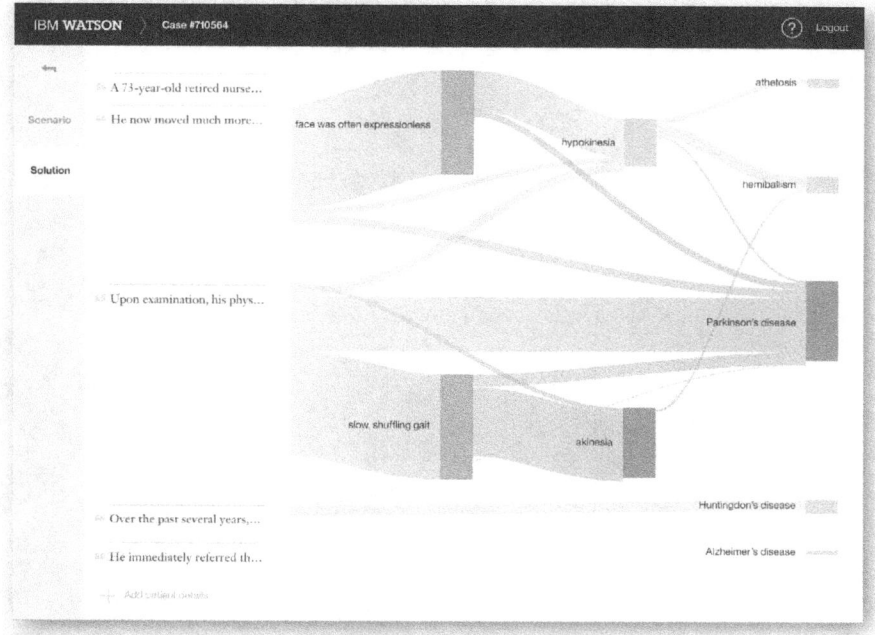

Figure 8: IBM Watson Health—Diagnosis

Inconsistency and human error are still large and common problems among physicians and medical professionals, no matter how many years of experience they have. Doctors are just normal human beings, and there is always room for human error. Imagine how difficult it is for doctors to keep up with the latest research and developments in their field of practice. Watson can hold much more information than doctors can, and he never overlooks or forgets anything, which secures high accuracy and consistency in every diagnosis. Watson can go to work everywhere in the world and support doctors without any traveling time, as he only needs Internet access to be ready for a call.

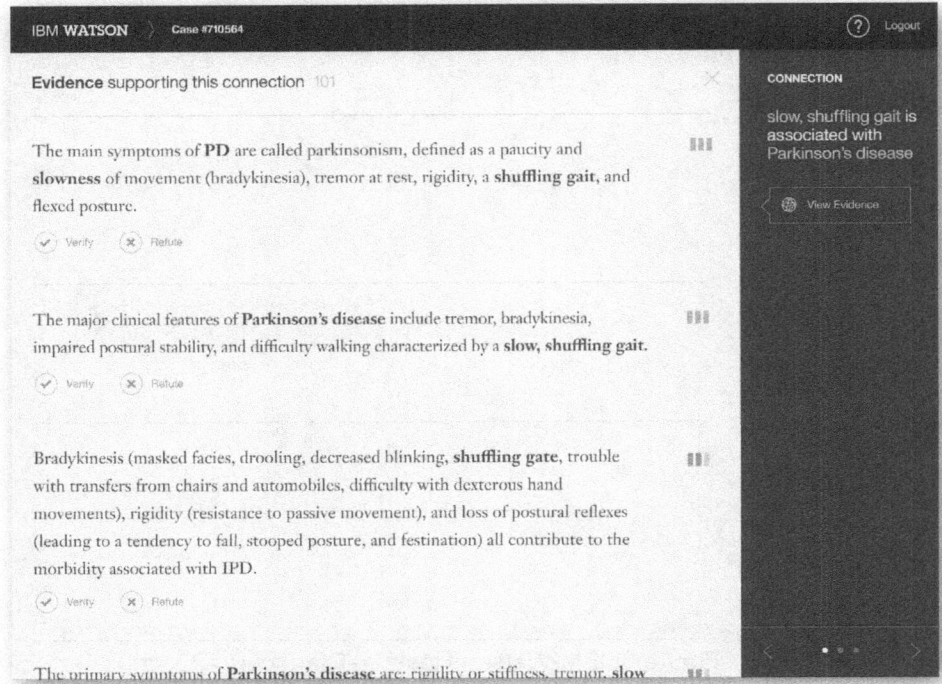

Figure 9: IBM Watson Health—Evidence for Diagnosis

IBM Watson as Your New Chef in the Kitchen

Besides Watson's analytical capabilities, Watson can also be creative, like in the case of IBM's Chef Watson. The cooking magazine *Bon Appétit* worked with IBM to develop an app that would create new recipes for cooking. To do this, *Bon Appétit* gave Watson access to its large (over ten thousand) recipe database to learn what works well together. Watson now uses this data to invent new recipes, and he learns from the feedback he gets from app users. An article from *Bon Appétit* explains the process this way: "Watson searches for patterns in the existing recipes and combines them with an extensive knowledge of the science behind food pairings to come up with ideas for unexpected combinations. For example, a braise always requires an initial sear and low-and-slow cooking with liquid. Watson socked away that information and added its knowledge of the chemical compounds that would make good ingredient pairings to inspire braises with brand-new flavors."[12]

The recipes can inspire both home cooks and chefs in fine restaurants. For over a year now, chefs of *Bon Appétit* have been trying out Chef Watson's recipes in their kitchens and publishing the results as new recipe suggestions for readers. The results are thrilling and, in this case, very tasty. You can try it out yourself, since IBM Chef Watson has recently become publicly available on www.ibmchefwatson.com.

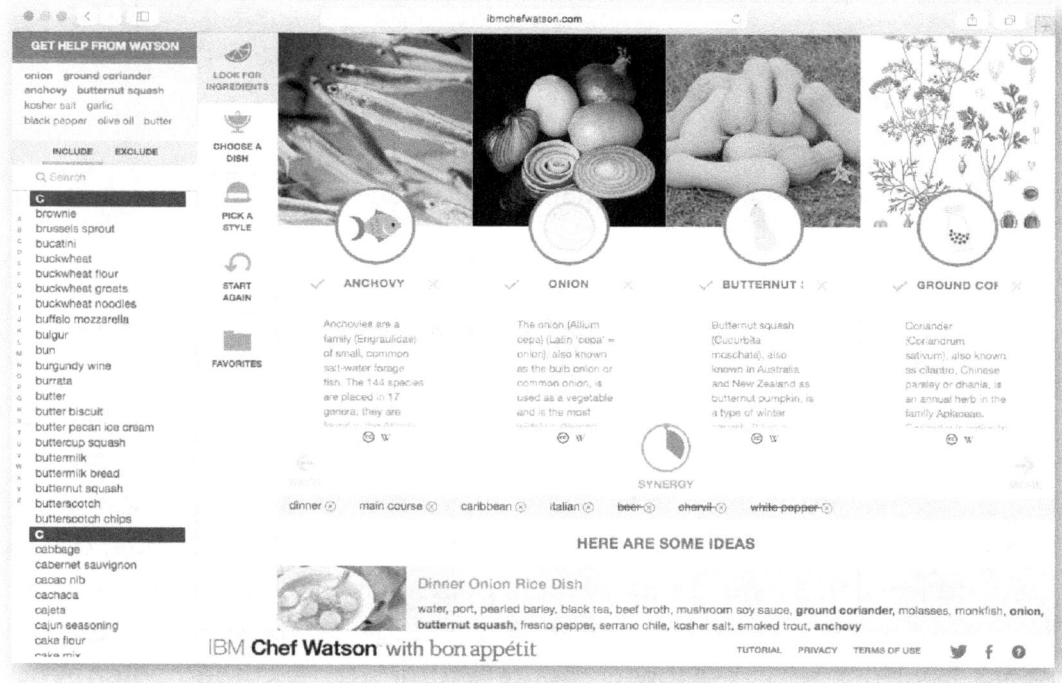

Figure 10: IBM Chef Watson

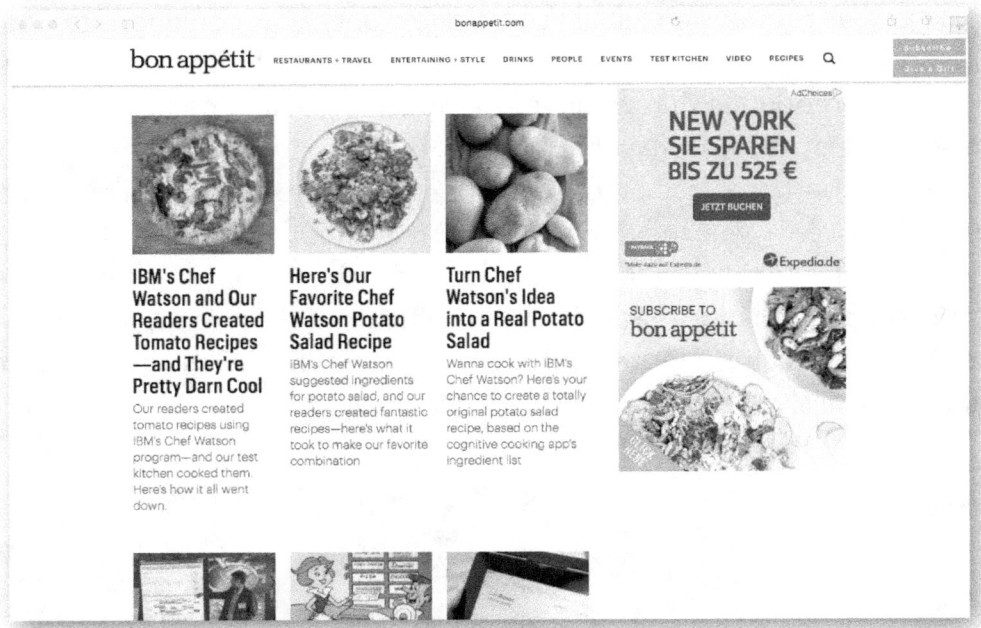

Figure 11: Bon Appétit Watson

Everyone Can Now Use Watson via APIs for Their Marketing Innovations

Today Watson is available for everyone as software as a service via application program interfaces (APIs) and can be used for many innovations in marketing. A large variety of services are available (see Figure 12). Language services include text analysis, natural language dialogue, document conversion, language translation, personality analysis, and customer sentiment analysis. Speech services include speech to text and text to speech. Vision services allow computers to understand the content and context of a picture, analyze which pictures your customers are looking at, and even understand the content of videos. Data insights services enable developers to collect news on particular topics across the Internet and provide a decision-support engine that is based on game theory. The example of cognitive marketing with Opentopic described below utilizes Watson APIs as part of the overall application.

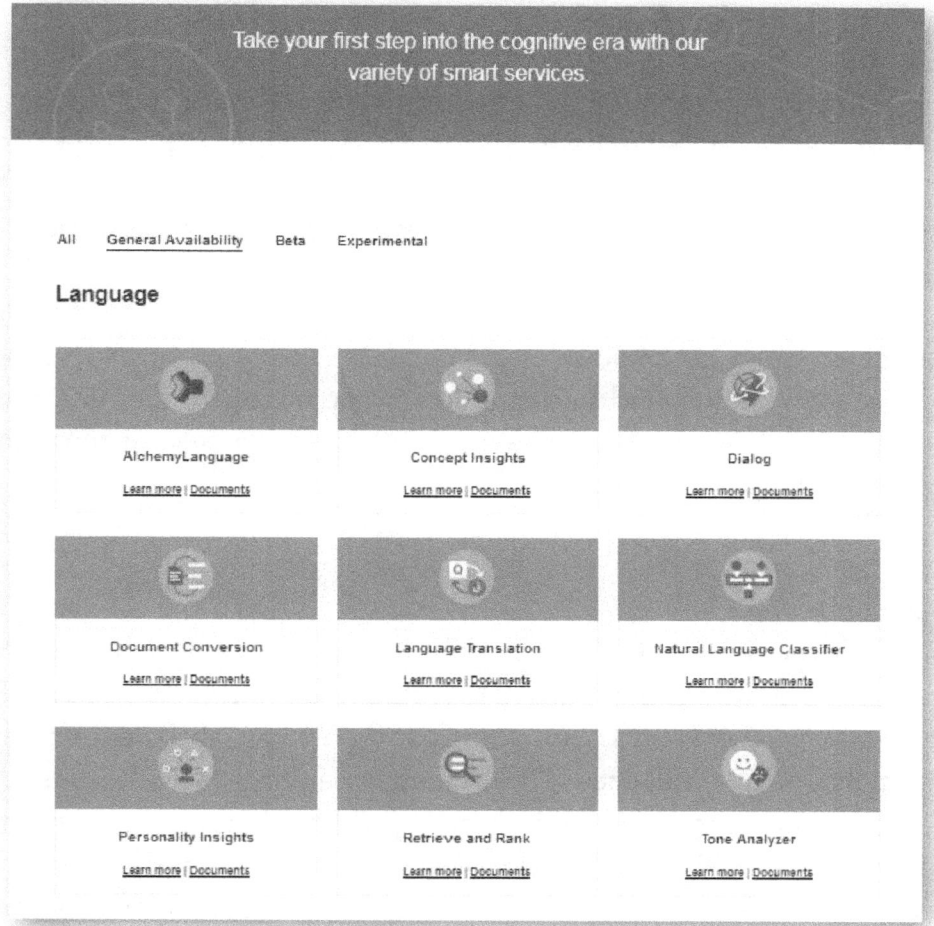

Figure 12: IBM Watson Developer Cloud

Cognitive Digital Marketing by Opentopic

A New York City–based start-up called Opentopic is combining two of the leading trends in marketing: personalized engagement and content marketing. Their solution enables marketing managers to deliver relevant and precise content and marketing campaigns for any given target audience.

Higher Conversion Rates for E-Commerce Sites

One of the in-practice examples for Opentopic is SoundGear, which is an online hub and e-commerce platform for music makers. SoundGear wants to deliver value for passionate customers by combining the most relevant instrument/production-related content to its product range. Instead of presenting boring product descriptions, it can excite customers with fascinating real-life stories from leading artists, professionals, and fans. This allows a much deeper engagement with the audience and helps to better present the possibilities of the products sold. Opentopic is helping SoundGear to define and understand its audience, source, and target-relevant content, improving conversion and success measures through automated learning.

Audience Insight

One of the key differentiators of Opentopic is its capability to understand audiences. Opentopic leverages IBM Watson's cognitive APIs[13] to perform trend analysis, understand connections and patterns, and create comprehensive insight on audiences. This involves analyzing vast amounts of unstructured data from news feeds, blogs, and websites, mostly in the form of text. Watson then identifies trending topics, assesses the topic significance, and provides a confidence interval on the topic relevancy for the defined audience. Based on the page impressions and conversion rates for the content, Watson then learns and adapts its algorithms by machine learning. In addition, human experts help Watson to improve on the preciseness by rating suggested content, therefore increasing the confidence interval.

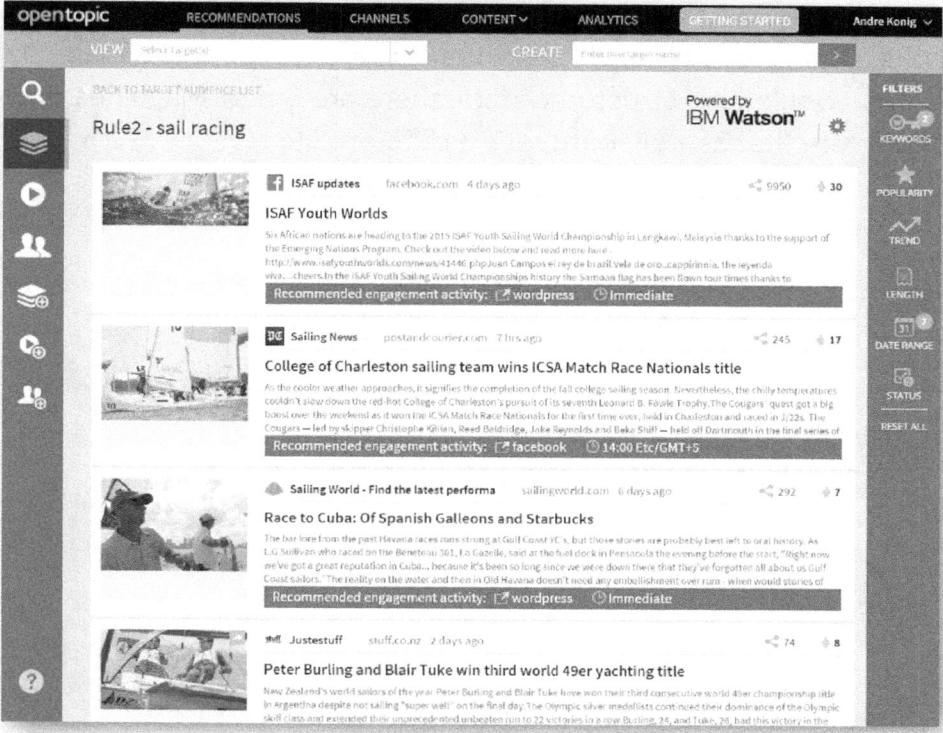

Figure 13: Opentopic Example

Automated Insights Create Machines That Write

The value proposition of Automated Insights is very simple: "generate un-limited pieces of content from a single story structure and dataset that sounds like a person wrote each one of them individually."[14] Their solution, called Wordsmith, involves converting data into articles, reports, web pages, and other forms of content. This makes it much easier for the recipient to understand the message, product, offer, or trend.

How to Make an Automated Property Description

Let's get to work with Wordsmith on writing a description of an available rental flat.[15] First, we need to upload the data in a structured format, like an Excel table. The table below shows the typical information required to make a statement on a property that's available for rent or sale. By the way, if you don't have structured data, there are Smart Machines that can help you with that as well, but that's a different story.

bathrooms	bedrooms	year_built	num_floors	house_style
4	3.5	2007	1	Craftsman
3	2	1961	1	Bungalow
4	2	2004	1	Ranch
4	2	1930	2	Craftsman
3	2.5	1900	1	Ranch
2	2	1942	2	Bungalow
3	2	2008	2	Cape Cod
2	1.5	1946	2	Modern
3	1.5	1937	2	Craftsman
4	3	1900	1	Bungalow

Figure 14: Wordsmith Input Table Example

Second, we need to design the article by defining narratives using the editor tool. This is the step where we make connections between the different table columns and define the length, tone, and variability of the article to make it unique and personalized.

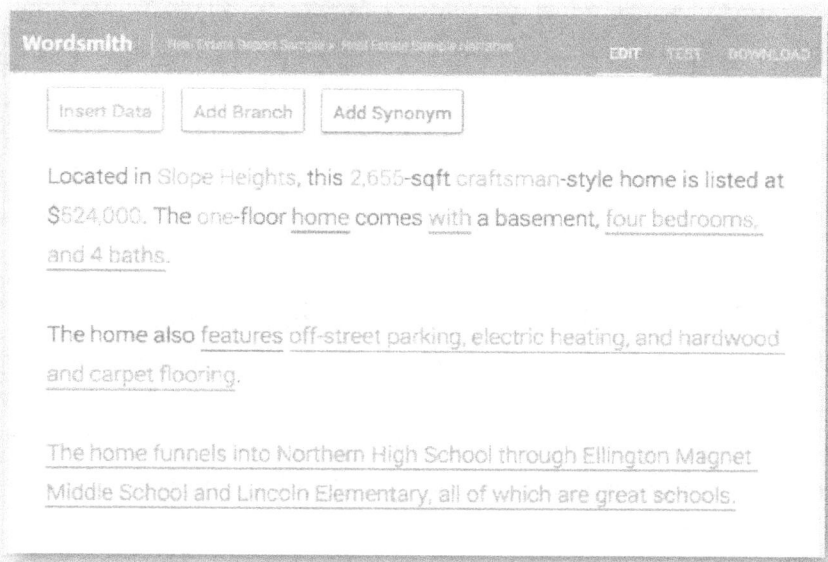

Figure 15: Wordsmith Design Your Article Example

Third, we need to generate our narratives and let the machine write the description of the property. Below you see the final output.

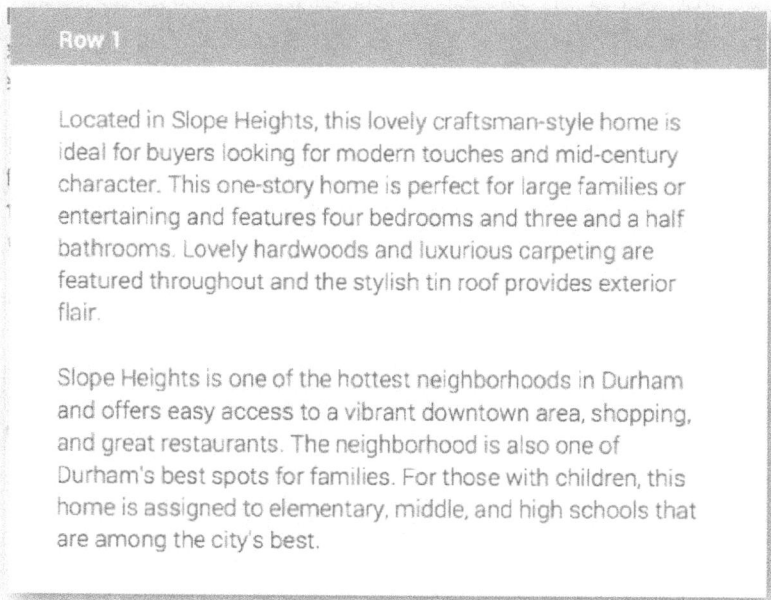

Figure 16: Wordsmith Output Text Example

The example shows how easy it is to write good content and to scale humanlike communication. Although Automated Insight is working with predefined models for now, the future will bring fully automated text creation by Smart Machines, which require less input from humans on defining standards.

What's Next and How Do We Get There?

There is no better proof than real-world examples that our world is speeding toward an algorithmic economy based on Smart Machines with advanced cognitive capabilities. We admit there is still a long way to go before we see Smart Machines as naturally integrated as they are in our story of a day in a life of a marketeer ten years from now. As many disruptive shifts have shown us in the past, things will not happen overnight. But they accelerate as soon as people realize how to apply new capabilities and when the cost for implementing and using those capabilities comes down through economies of scale. The next chapter will take a closer look at the capabilities and drivers of Smart Machines and the data-driven algorithmic economy.

Part II

The Forces Behind

Chapter 5

Omnipresent: How Smart Machines Sense

All our knowledge begins with the senses.

—IMMANUEL KANT

Data, Data, Everywhere

In the past, the physical world and the digital world were quite disconnected, as only a small proportion of information in the physical world was captured digitally. This will certainly change in the future. Data about nearly anything in the physical world will be captured electronically and hence digitized. Within the first decade of the twenty-first century, the number of people connected to the Internet grew from 350 million to more than two billion. In the same period, the number of mobile phone subscribers grew from 750 million to over five billion, reaching the farthest places on our planet.[16]

Until now we have seen more and more data about our lives being captured on social media—human knowledge being shared on the Internet, but also information being exchanged to organize business and life. Within a few years, the Internet could see over half a billion people using social network platforms like Facebook, MySpace, and LinkedIn on a daily basis to communicate with their friends, colleagues, and business contacts. One study states that one out of every seven minutes spent online is spent on Facebook alone,[17] and 40 percent of people socialize more online than they do face to face.[18]

Today a large proportion of information contains social information around private and professional lives: feelings and emotions, photos and videos, and things that people "like." This large amount of data adds a new dimension to understanding customers and consumers. Social data can be used to complement existing customer relationship management (CRM) corporate data to achieve a greater understanding of customers. For instance, Twitter data can reveal what customers think about the organization and its products and services, as well as provide an understanding of which issues affect the organization's reputation. Platforms like Facebook and LinkedIn can provide a richer picture of customers and customer segments, their social network, and their personal preferences. It is important for organizations to tap into this rich new source of quite personal information without offending customers and employees.

* Every day 2.5 quintillion bytes of data are created. Ninety percent of the world's data has been created in the past two years alone.[19]

Data captured by humans will be increasingly outnumbered by data created by machines. Sensors built into cars, household appliances, and even human bodies (e.g., for health monitoring) will digitalize a much larger proportion of the information from the physical world in the years to come. Research company IDC estimates that the number of connected things is already approaching two hundred billion, and the number of sensors that track, monitor, or feed data to those things is already more than fifty billion.[20] Data can increasingly be captured digitally in all parts of real life by ubiquitous computing systems armed with different types of wireless sensors, data logs, cameras, mobile devices, GPS, microphones, or RFID tags (to name a few). "The Internet of things" is a buzz phrase coined by researchers at the Massachusetts Institute of Technology to describe the increasing digitization of the real world.[21] We will see sensors and chips being integrated more and more often into our "normal"—which means nondigital—lives. For example, our refrigerator will become more intelligent in the future; it will know what foods and drinks it contains, when perishables expire, and which items are running low. Our car will automatically know which replacement parts it needs. Our own health may be monitored using sensors and chips strapped to the body.

The different data sources are becoming better interconnected around the world, often in real time, and data is exchanged at rapid speeds between people and machines that are able to speak to and understand one another. New standards are developing in all areas of life and business to make data more easily exchangeable, and instant translation of languages removes barriers of communication across borders. Computers are also better at handling and connecting data from different sources and making the data compatible. Many new things will become possible through that interconnectivity. For example, the integrated information captured by smartphones of the citizens living in a particular city, for instance, could be used to find patterns in movement to optimize traffic and public transport, and to distribute information about which routes are the best to use in real time to end consumers on their mobile devices. People will be able to work in virtual teams that are distributed across the planet. Top Google executives Eric Schmidt and Jared Cohen bring it to the point: "As global connectivity continues its unprecedented advance, many old institutions will have to adapt or risk becoming obsolete, irrelevant to modern society."[22]

The Five Senses of Smart Machines

Imagine the countless possibilities if machines were able to see, hear, smell, taste, and touch. In the next age of computing, Smart Machines will develop human brain–like capabilities that are based on the ability to emulate the five human senses.

Seeing Machines

Machines are able to see through optical character recognition, video and image recognition, and text recognition. Those capabilities are already used in many state-of-the-art cars to support driver safety and traffic security. Image-processing technology tracks the movement of a driver's eyes, face, head, and facial expression to monitor driver fatigue and distraction events in real time. Those advanced driver assistance systems (ADAS) will alert the driver or process intervention strategies to improve driver and environmental safety. This could mean that it automatically pushes audio or vibration alerts, reduces driving speed, and posts outside safety signals.

Hearing Machines

Machines are able to take in and process sound data such as music, speech, sounds of nature, and sounds of machines. In an interview with *MIT Technology Review*, the engineer Paris Smaragdis explained key characteristics of hearing machines, referring to them as "software that uses sound to locate people moving through rooms, monitor machinery for impending breakdowns, or activate traffic cameras to record accidents."[23] One remarkable example of machine listening comes from the start-up Augury's Gadget, a device that lets machines hear when they are about to fail. Similar to a Formula One driver who notices even little changes in the noise of an engine, Augury's Gadget records vibrations and ultrasonic sound and permanently sends it to Augury's cloud, where it is analyzed against machine patterns to predict the state of the machine. This enables better, faster, and more accurate decisions on preventive maintenance and repairs.

Feeling Machines

Machines are able to identify objects by touch, similar to human tactile sensing. This ability is fueled by technological innovations around tactile sensors, which convert information from physical interactions into data.

Tactile sensing can be defined as "the process of detecting and measuring a given property of a contact event in a predetermined area and subsequent processing of the signal—before sending them to higher levels for perceptual interpretation."[24] Tactile sensing is used in many different fields of applications, including, for example, in biomedicine, human-robot interaction, rehabilitation, and prosthetics.

One of the most advanced uses of tactile sensors is in the field of minimally invasive surgery. Tactile sensing by machines will allow surgeons to make smaller incisions and use sensors to virtually feel and look at a patient's internal organs. Highly advanced tactile sensors could even differentiate cancerous cells from healthy cells.

Tasting Machines

Machines are able to taste the five basic tastes: sour, salty, bitter, sweet, and umami. However, basic tastes might be simpler to detect compared to the richness of flavors that are a complex mixture of taste, smell, texture, temperature, and chemesthesis. Technological advancements and innovations will increase the tasting capabilities of Smart Machines. In addition, machine learning will allow a fast adoption to more complex tastes and flavors.

Smelling Machines

Machines are able to smell just like our human nose does. In order to smell, sensors gather data from the smell of air by detecting chemicals and other particles (similar to how a breathalyzer can determine alcohol levels). They can also detect substances that humans cannot smell through their noses. Imagine if your smartphone knew that you were going to get a cold before you did by detecting chemicals that you cannot. We are in the early stages of using machines to identify patterns indicating cancer and other diseases. Machines will be able to prescribe what is needed to prevent diseases and improve nutrition, thus improving the overall health and vitality of our bodies.

Combining the Senses

Every human sense in itself can create feelings and experiences. But the magic of combining and activating multiple senses is what gets human beings excited, deeply touched, enthusiastic, and frightened. The human brain connects all senses to create or trigger a meaningful response. The more Smart Machines can connect data from multiple senses, the more they can correlate patterns to multiple input factors. You might be surprised by the findings, which totally change some underlying perceptions of experiences and emotions.

> ★ Finding the needle in the haystack is a major challenge when so much sensed data is available to be processed.

Ultimately, machines will become omnipresent, which means that they can listen and speak, observe and show, and feel and touch wherever you are. It means that machines get senses to perceive the world and the ability to communicate and act in many ways.

Yes, there will hopefully still be some wild parts of our planet remaining where machines do not have eyes and ears. But unless you live in very special places like Kyrgyzstan (an ex-Soviet country with a lot of stunning nature in a vastly empty land), it is likely that machines will be omnipresent in your everyday life in a few years' time.

How Smart Machines Process Sensed Data

Not all the information we collect with our human senses is actually stored in our brain. There is too much noise, and we would be overwhelmed if we had to make meaningful responses to each one. Our brain is trained to distinguish information that is important to us from amid all the noise that we capture. Therefore, machines need to develop "noise reduction" capabilities—or at least they have to learn them.

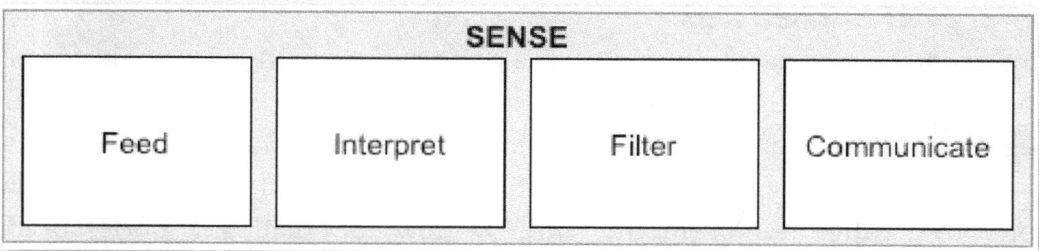

Figure 17: How Smart Machines Sense

Feed New Data

With the rise of connected devices, vast amounts of digital data feeds, and new forms of data providers, companies need to process tremendous amounts of internal and external data, and most of the data needs to be processed in real time or near real time. Application programming interfaces (APIs) are the connectors of what many already call the API economy. Many of those APIs are based on triggers and responses. Relevant real-time triggers for marketing are, for example, ad clicks, social media posts, shopping cart abandons, and location-based alerts that lead to immediate responses such as promotional coupons, targeted ads, branded content, or simply remote support. Those feeds could come from owned media sources like a native app or third-party providers like Facebook. Most of the incoming data will also trigger data published to external partners or other internal sources, where it is used to generate further insights—for example, by enriching customer profiles or behavior patterns.

A few years from now, companies will process and analyze data in real time independent of source or process. The challenge for companies is to be connected to the relevant data or in some cases even identify valuable data or data sources. Smart Machines will especially help the marketing function to identify new data sources or areas of interest.

Interpret Sensed Data

Interpretation of data, which today is done mostly by human analysts, will be taken over by Smart Machines. This requires new processing capabilities around connecting data points, understanding and assessing patterns, and formulating hypotheses, which then will be tested fully automatically or with creative human input. With the new capabilities of understanding unstructured data in the form of text, images, and audio files, Smart Machines can now draw a comprehensive and consolidated picture of the physical world as well as of the digital world. New data algorithms will be required to either automatically process data for further structuring or enrich data with information that is not naturally available in the process. Data enrichment in particular is currently done manually or through semi-automated processes. Smart Machines need to be able to enrich data and combine different data sets from different sources to improve data exploration and pattern recognition.

Filter Out the Noise

The brain constantly filters out unimportant details to reduce the neural input from the environment. Our senses create an enormous amount of data that needs to get processed. Why don't we get overwhelmed by all the inputs? The area of the brain that helps us to filter the noise is the thalamus. It helps us to orchestrate the sensed information and to focus on the most important things in the moment. Smart Machines require the same kind of mechanism to direct the flow of data and trigger the right actions. Data filtering and synthesizing is a core capability of Smart Machines and is one area where marketing needs to build up competencies and experts, as this is currently outside of a typical marketing working focus.

Communicate with Other Smart Machines and Humans

Machine-to-machine (M2M) communication is one of the fastest-growing areas of data and information exchange. Most of the communication and related actions are fully automated or autonomous, without any human intervention. Moreover, the communication has emerged into a system of networks combining connected devices. This allows not only the capture and analysis of data but also the ability to push direct feedback or actions to end users, customers, or robots.

Remote services by Smart Machines or performed by workers with the help of Google Glass provide a window into the future of seamlessly integrated networks of devices, Smart Machines, systems, and humans. This will require various combinations of the above described capabilities of feeding, interpreting, and filtering data. Developing intelligent algorithms around those capabilities will be a great source of competitive advantage, as it enables the core flow of information, the triggers of actions, and the discovery of patterns. On the other hand, communication with humans will be based on cognitive capabilities, meaning that machines will communicate like humans through a voice interface.

Our "In Practice" articles present some leading practices on how Smart Machines can come closer to the five human senses.

In Practice: Tell me what's inside my drink[25]

In recent years, smartphones have evolved into our personal companions. They give us directions on where to go next, connect us to our friends, sense our motion, and help us to capture our experiences as pictures. What if they could also tell you what your food or drink is made of? A recent invention by Tel Aviv University professor David Mendlovic and doctoral student Ariel Raz promises to answer exactly this question. Their invention is based on a microelectromechanical optical component that functions as a miniature filter that allows smartphone cameras to take hyperspectral images. These images store the spectrum of light within every pixel of the image. Their software then produces a spectral map and compares it to a database with spectral maps of substances. The result is fascinating. If you take a simple picture of a cocktail, the smartphone can tell you the composition of the liquid. This isn't just a lot of fun; it also allows endless new opportunities. It could track your nutrition, inform you of unhealthy ingredients (e.g., for people with allergies), or help you to identify all the ingredients for the meal you just had in a restaurant. It might also be used as a safety feature to warn workers of dangerous liquids or substances. In general, the example shows how advanced sensors have become to sense and analyze the environment around us using consumer devices such as smartphones.

Figure 18: Pioneering Mobile Hyperspectral Imaging (Source: http://www.ramot.org/media-center/video-gallery/ramot/media/26889)

In Practice: Millions of colors in your hand[26]

As sensors are getting increasingly cheaper and better, more and more devices have embedded sensors that not only sense and capture information but also trigger immediate responses. The Scribble color-matching pen is able to recognize a color and then allow the user to draw in that same color. You take a real painting and you can start drawing directly on real paper or on your tablet. With its replaceable nib and six tip sizes, Scribble reproduces over sixteen million colors in multiple stroke weights. That's enough to repaint the most beautiful paintings in the world!

In Practice: Old McDonald has a farm with the tagged cow #10III0IP7

More and more consumers are concerned about the quality and the origin of what they eat. Today consumers need to trust the labeling and quality controls performed by companies and authorities. However, it is very difficult to judge the individual quality of products across the entire value chain. Wearables and ingestible sensors for animals have the power to change that, and one of the leading companies in this space is iNOVO-TECH. Their ingestible devices are, for example, recording the pH levels in the stomach and the body temperature of the animal. The captured data enables farmers to better understand parameters affecting the health of their animals, to identify and treat diseases or ailments, and to receive alerts in case of a needed feed change. From a marketing perspective, the power of the data lies in creating more transparency and differentiation in the value chain from the farm to the end consumer. Consumers will be able to scan the packaging of the meat they buy and then get information about where the meat came from, which farm produced it, and the health of the animals on the farm. Companies can then offer products based on the preferences of the consumer.

From Sensing to Thinking and Learning

The capability to see, hear, smell, taste, and feel is as important for Smart Machines as it is for human beings. Those senses are the "interface" with the real world and help paint the picture of what's happening out there. Now that Smart Machines can sense the world, in our next chapter we will look at how they reason and learn, as this really differentiates Smart Machines from intelligent sensors.

Chapter 6

•   •   •

Cognitive: How Smart Machines Think and Learn

I think, therefore I am.

—RENÉ DESCARTES

Thank you...you said "someone"...not "something."

—SONNY, IN THE MOVIE *I, ROBOT*

The Essential Capability

Machines that think are a somewhat frightening idea. In the eyes of many humans, thinking is the only capability that truly differentiates us from other animals and computers. We have discussed the six senses of Smart Machines. In this chapter we introduce the most important ability of Smart Machines: to process the sensed information similar to the way we humans process information (i.e., via empirical learning).

Smart Machines are able to:

* understand the meaning of natural language and of images, speech, videos, etc.;
* link sensed data to the existing knowledge base and make associations;
* discover patterns and generate and evaluate hypotheses to find answers to questions;
* decide to collect more data and reiterate to increase the level of confidence;
* provide answers in natural language and justify the conclusions; and
* learn from experience without reprogramming to increase the knowledge base.

Those characteristics are the basis for building your own cognitive applications with Smart Machines that can author personalized and contextualized content, provide assistance and advice to your customers, manage your marketing campaigns, automatically determine the best price levels for your services and products (even under very unstable external conditions), and even generate ideas for new customized products. The ability of Smart Machines to think and learn is, thus, a key driver for the algorithmic economy. This chapter explains the basis for such applications: the concepts and mechanisms that allow a Smart Machine to think and learn.

Understanding How Humans Think and Learn

Science has not fully deciphered the memory and cognitive activities of a human brain due to its immense complexity.[28] We only have a basic understanding of our brain functions. On a very simplified level, our five senses provide new information about the world, stored in our sensorial memory. The short-term memory processes some of this new information selectively when it seems to be relevant. To interpret this new information, our short-term memory uses the knowledge of our long-term memory and makes associations. For instance, when we read, the short-term memory uses the long-term memory (from when we learned how to read in school) to translate the images of characters into natural language. In contrast, assuming we cannot read Chinese symbols, our brain does not have the knowledge of how to interpret these characters. Whenever our brain deems something important enough, it is stored in our long term memory.

⋆ Human cognition applies two different systems: fast thinking and slow thinking.

According to Daniel Kahneman (a Nobel Prize winner in economics for his behavioral economics theory, jointly developed with Amos Tversky), humans have two systems with which to process new information.[29] The first system, "fast thinking," is rule based and operates automatically and with little effort (e.g., locating the source of a sudden sound, reading words in a language we know well, or driving a car on an empty road). The second system, "slow thinking," requires a lot of effort in order to make complex computations as it observes and tests assumptions and creates new rules. In essence, system two learns new knowledge, while system one applies this knowledge.

Knowledge can be procedural. Not closing the eyes when putting in contact lenses for the first time is extremely challenging because of our inborn blinking reflex, which is executed by system one. It takes a lot of effort and some time for system two to teach system one not to automatically shut your eye when putting in the lens.

As we learn, our long-term memory can gather different types of knowledge.[30] *Declarative knowledge* includes facts and their interrelationships (i.e., semantic memory and facts about the world) and events (i.e., episodic memory and the capacity to reexperience an event in the context in which it originally occurred) to help to model the external world. This is what we typically call "memory" in our everyday language. However, as a result of learning, we can also create *nondeclarative knowledge*, such as skills, habits, reflexes, and emotional responses that change the rules of how system one reacts to impulses. This type of knowledge is formed gradually by extracting the common elements from a series of separate events.

Maybe you have seen the Hollywood movie *Transcendence*, in which Johnny Depp's brain is copied into a Smart Machine to extend his own human life. Although cognitive machines share many of the principles of how a human brain works, this does not mean they work the same way. In particular, how humans feel emotions is very unique and hard to imitate. So luckily, it is doubtful that Smart Machines will be able to do what was portrayed in the movie anytime in the near future.

What Makes a Machine Cognitive?

The word *cognitive* comes from psychology. Cognitive psychology is the study of the mental processes of humans, such as "attention, language use, memory, perception, problem solving, creativity, and thinking."[31] Computers have always been pretty good at repetitive and clearly described tasks and in applying strict logic and complex mathematics. An abundance of tasks today is solved by computers much more quickly, cheaply, and reliably than by humans. Yet in many ways computers oftentimes appear annoyingly stupid. Have you tried to have a meaningful and interesting conversation with a computer? It can be a difficult and typically very frustrating endeavor.

What computers are missing is the *ability to understand the meaning* of what we have to say. This is because language is very ambiguous. The very same sentence can mean something completely opposite if said in another situation or by a different person. "I love this computer" could mean "I really like my computer a lot," or it could mean "I really hate my computer because it doesn't do what I want it to do." It is very unlikely that "love" refers to romantic love in this context.

The idea that computers can think like a human sounds like a stretch; it is, however, closer than you might think with the rise of *cognitive computing*.

★ Cognitive computing goes beyond the computer we used to know: somehow intelligent when problems are very logical and mathematical, and often very dumb when it comes to everyday problems. Smart Machines can handle situations with ambiguity, sparse information, and uncertainty and thus are able to solve human kinds of problems.

Cognitive computing makes machines better able to handle situations with ambiguity, sparse information, and uncertainty and thus able to solve human kinds of problems. Instead of calculating the optimal solution using a predefined algorithm, Smart Machines evaluate different options and choose the best option out of the possibilities. Problems do not need to be provided in a specified machine-readable format; they can be simply formulated in natural language or even normal speech. Looking at the context of the problem makes it possible to interpret the question correctly. When I ask a Smart Machine, "What is the best restaurant?" it should understand that I am probably looking for a good restaurant that is not too far away from my current location.

Based on the outcomes of an action, Smart Machines can learn and improve their problem solving. Instead of being programmed, they can read documents to understand a business process and observe how humans perform that process to build its own knowledge base and eventually be able to handle the business process on its own. A key characteristic is that a cognitive system can recognize which questions it needs to ask; thus, it is interactive. In the given example, if the system is unsure how far I am willing to walk or whether I am willing to take a taxi, it could ask me, "How far away can the restaurant be? Are you planning to walk or take a cab?" It also understands needs that are not clearly communicated. For example, it could proactively advise me to take the metro instead of a taxi because it is faster due to the current traffic situation.

Finally, Smart Machines have a real memory. If I tell the Smart Machine that I generally do not like to go to Tex-Mex restaurants but I do like authentic

Mexican cuisine, it should remember this when I next ask for a restaurant recommendation. This all sounds pretty impressive for machines, doesn't it?

The Key Components of a Smart Machine

Smart Machines have the ability to solve problems in a similar way to humans because they can think and learn in a similar way to a human. Like the human brain, a cognitive machine is a system of systems, and each system plays its essential role in thinking and learning. Each of the components will be examined in the next sections in more detail.

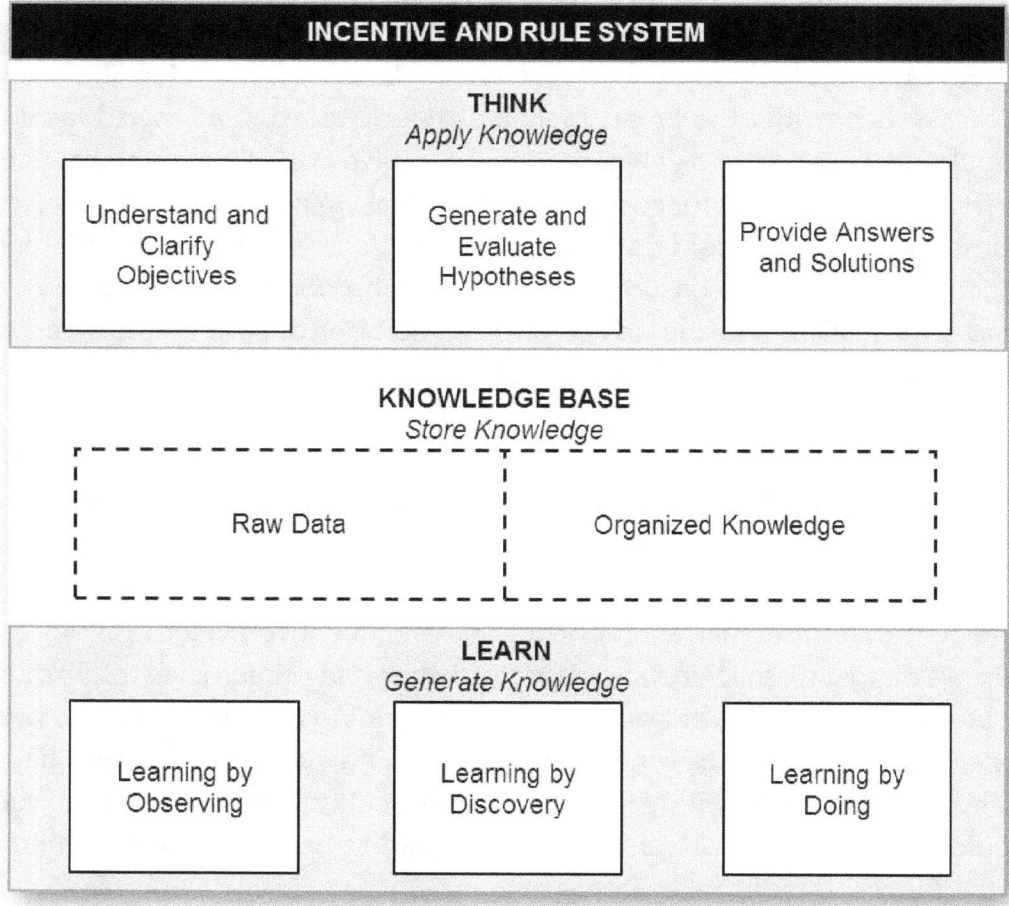

Figure 19: How Smart Machines Think and Learn

Designing the Incentive and Rule System

Smart Machines have certain goals that can be set, such as providing an answer with the highest possible confidence based on evidence. When we humans have to solve a difficult task, we need a motivation to do that. Our human brain incentivizes us by releasing endorphins that make us feel happy when we are successful at something or when we are rewarded. This positive experience makes us try harder next time. Although Smart Machines do not have feelings, they do need a way to recognize whether they are doing the right thing or not. Setting targets is therefore an essential part of incentivizing a Smart Machine. In a way, you can compare this to a briefing given by your boss on what you are supposed to achieve during the next calendar year.

So what would the right incentive system be for a Smart Machine? Well, it depends on what the Smart Machines needs to do. If a Smart Machine should play the role of a call-center agent to give advice on different types of mortgage products for customers who are planning to build a house, the number of products sold could be the metric used to incentivize a Smart Machine. Additional measures might include the percentage of customers who are satisfied with the advice and the number of calls that needed to be escalated to a human agent.

* A Smart Machine is built for a particular purpose and context. The incentives and rules need to be set in a way so that it fits the purpose and context.

The rule system is just as important as the incentive system. There are certain things the machine should not do under any circumstances (like tell your child to cross a street on a red light). Providing rules to a machine provides a safety net to prevent misbehavior, unethical responses, and harm to humans, or it can simply help it adhere to cultural norms. A simple rule could be that a Smart Machine is not allowed to use swear words when it provides responses to a customer.

How Smart Machines Think

The ability to think makes it possible for Smart Machines to deal with unclear and constantly changing goals. This ability can be divided in three parts: understanding a new instruction or question posed by a human (or even another machine), generating and testing hypotheses, and providing answers and solutions.

Understand and Clarify Objectives

Smart Machines do not need to be reprogrammed when the tasks they need to perform change. Instead you give them a new instruction or problem to solve. For instance, in a near-future scenario, you will be able to give your household robot the instruction that the thermostat needs to be adapted to your presence at home. The robot needs to deconstruct the instruction into its elements and interpret what you really mean by it: that the heat needs to be turned on in time for the house to be warm when you or your family arrive home, and the rest of the time (when everyone is out of the home), the heat should be turned off to save energy. Still, there might be open questions, so the robot might need to clarify the instruction by asking a question of you, such as "What is the temperature you would like when you are at home?"

When there is a question, it needs to be similarly deconstructed and interpreted by finding patterns and making associations in the knowledge base and linking sensed data to understand the context of the question. An example could be that you ask your Smart Machine about the best way to get to the airport. The "best way" could mean many things. It could be the fastest way, the cheapest way, or the most convenient way to the airport. What is clear is that you need to be in time for the airplane and that there is a particular airport you need to be at. So the machine checks your current location and the boarding time and departing airport on your boarding pass (stored in your smartphone) and might ask you about your preferences for transportation.

Generate and Evaluate Hypotheses

A distinct feature of Smart Machines is that they can generate and evaluate hypotheses to find answers to questions or solutions to problems. A *hypothesis* is defined by the Oxford English Dictionary as "a supposition or proposed explanation made on the basis of limited evidence as a starting point for further investigation." The key characteristic for a hypothesis is that it needs to be testable. Creating and testing a hypothesis is important, as it gives you the ability to handle uncertainty and information that is sparse and ambiguous. Based on the interpretation of a problem statement, one or several hypotheses are generated by discovering patterns and potential solutions within the knowledge base.

For example, if the objective is to find a treatment for a patient who shows a set of symptoms, the hypotheses could be that the symptoms are connected to three potential diseases. At this point in time, there is not enough evidence for the Smart Machine to decide if the hypotheses are true or untrue and if the solution is the right one or not. They are all solution candidates and need to be tested against further evidence that has to be collected. Data from different sources might need to be acquired and interpreted and then tested if the hypothesis is supported by the data. If the level of confidence is high enough to support one of the hypotheses, a solution is provided. In the previous example, the three diseases that might be connected to the symptoms are potential candidates. The Smart Machine would collect evidence from its knowledge base (e.g., research papers on diseases, ISO classification of illnesses, and past diagnoses and treatments) and would evaluate and score each candidate based on the evidence.

Provide Answers and Solutions

Finally, the Smart Machine need to evaluate which hypotheses are most likely the right ones based on the scoring and the overall answer or solution to a problem. If there is enough supporting evidence for one or more hypotheses to defend a solution, the solution is found. The Smart Machine can provide these answers in natural language and justify the conclusions with evidence and a level of confidence. Otherwise Smart Machines can decide to collect more data and reiterate to increase the level of confidence or even come up with further new hypotheses that can be tested to find a better-fitting solution.

In the medical example, there might be enough evidence that one particular disease is connected to the symptoms observed. It could also happen that the Smart Machine would ask the doctor to perform another examination or test to detail or identify further symptoms and evidence. The doctor is then informed about the most likely disease (including the supporting evidence and likelihood), and the best treatment options connected to this disease are suggested to the doctor.

How Smart Machines Build a Knowledge Base

The knowledge base is the long-term memory of a Smart Machine. There is an important distinction between having a good memory of facts and being intelligent about them. Knowing millions of facts by heart (which we call "raw data" in this context) does not make you automatically intelligent unless you can understand and reason what these facts mean and how they are interrelated. For instance, having access to all Wikipedia articles provides computers with a lot of facts, but only cognitive computers are able to derive meaning from this text. Similar to humans, they can take new "raw data" and transform it into "organized knowledge" by building a *neural ontology* of the world, which consists of concepts and relationships between those concepts. Every new single piece of information that expands the current understanding of the world is integrated into the neural ontology by connecting it to the concepts that are already stored.

For example, if you first tell a Smart Machine that an iPhone is a mobile phone and then say that you own an iPhone, it would store the concept "iPhone" as a product name and build a relationship to the concept "smartphone" in its neural ontology. It would also store that fact that you have a phone called "iPhone" (concept "Your Name"—relationship "Owns"—concept "iPhone"). This allows a Smart Machine to store information in such a way that it can later derive meaning from the facts and respond to questions like "Which people do you know who own a smartphone?"

How Smart Machines Learn Passively and Actively

A key characteristic of Smart Machines is that they can learn. Machines can learn in three ways: by observation, by discovery, and by doing. Smart Machines can learn from experience to increase their own knowledge base without being reprogrammed, hence adapting and growing with their challenges over time.

★ As explained before, Smart Machines are not programmed. They are taught, teach themselves, or learn from their own experiences.

Learning by Observing

One way of learning is by observing how a human solves a task. When IBM Watson was trained to compete in the television quiz show *Jeopardy*, it was fed millions of question-and-answer pairs from previous shows. When IBM Watson was trained for the health-care industry to support doctors with diagnoses, it was fed millions of examples of real-life diagnoses that linked certain symptoms to a particular disease and showed the corresponding treatment that was recommended. When Smart Machine agents are trained to handle customer requests, like in the case of IPsoft's virtual assistant, Amelia, they learn from the behaviors of call-center agents by listening to actual phone calls with clients that were recorded for training purposes. This type of learning is also called *supervised learning* in the literature. The key behind supervised learning is that Smart Machines are provided with examples of how a problem was solved in real life.

Learning by Discovery

A second way Smart Machines learn is by discovery in the process of exploring data that is provided to them by their own experiences. When cooking, IBM Watson uses this way of learning to identify ingredients that fit well together to come up with new kinds of recipes. This type of learning is also known as *unsupervised learning.* Instead of getting question-and-answer pairs as described above, unsupervised learning provides computers with facts without showing how problems can be solved or how a solution can be found by using the facts. This type of learning works by identifying similarities and patterns in the data sets without having a target in mind.

For instance, supervised learning (by observation) would try to link symptoms to diseases, while unsupervised learning (by discovery) could just focus on identifying which symptoms often appear together. Discovery learning is needed in particular when problems are very complex and it is nearly impossible to show all combinations of questions and answers to a Smart Machine.

Learning by Doing

The third way of learning for Smart Machines is to learn by performing a task and then getting feedback if that task has been done well—hence, learning by doing. This is a very powerful way of learning. In fact, this is the way children learn many things they do later on as adults—by empiricism or, in simple terms, by trial and error. The concept behind this is quite simple. Imagine that a Smart Machine has to clean your room daily, and every time the machine completes the work, you rate the work using a green, yellow, or red button. The machine would learn over time what you like (and, more importantly, when you are dissatisfied) and could adapt the behavior to better fulfill your needs.

In Practice: When Smart Machines Turn Into Creative Artists

This is probably one of the most discussed questions on AI and Smart Machines. Can machines really be as creative as human beings? Hard to say, isn't it? Time will tell, but they are getting much better at creative tasks already. Here are some fascinating examples.

A Smart Machine called Iamus, the creation of computer scientist Francisco Vico and his collaborators at the University of Malaga in Spain, composes classical music.[32] The music cannot be distinguished from music composed by humans, even by musical experts. In 2012 some of the finest orchestras in the world, including the London Symphony Orchestra, performed the second album of Iamus.

The *New York Times* created an algorithm called Haiku, which checks newly published articles and creates poems out of them, as in the following:[33]

> *But they did not see*
> *any Trump Home mirrors or*
> *lotion dispensers.*

> *The auctioneers are*
> *addressed as "master," though they*
> *call themselves "hammers."*

The Creative Machines Lab at the Columbia University, led by Hod Lipson, is injecting creativity into machines. Their vision is to build biology-inspired machines that can evolve, self-model, and self-reflect, meaning they generate new ideas and make them reality. One of the most promising examples of creativity is PIX18, a robot that is able to paint oil on canvas. PIX18 is a standard factory robot that has been trained by the lab team to paint. Below you can see a painting from PIX18. What do you think? Would you be able to paint that picture?

Figure 20: Example of a Smart Machine Artwork (Source: http://www. hodlipson.com/uploads/6/9/3/4/69340277/1239079_orig.jpg)

From Knowing to Doing

The examples show that Smart Machines are becoming more creative and are getting closer to the ordinary human being, but machines are surely still far away from the creative capacity of Goethe, Picasso, or Mozart. The pace of improving the creativity of Smart Machines will depend not only on technological developments but also on the will of mankind to develop and master those skills in Smart Machines. For the near future, the key developments will still focus on lifting the think and learn capabilities that are essential to driving insight and impactful actions. In some areas of business and everyday life, we can already observe the first steps toward Smart Machines taking actions autonomously, and we will see even more progress over time.

Chapter 7

Autonomous: How Smart Machines Act

You are what you do, not what you say you'll do.

—C. G. JUNG

What Autonomous Means for Smart Machines

The ability to sense, think, and learn makes Smart Machines very intelligent, and intelligence is definitely valuable for any business. But the real impact is generated when actions result from intelligence. This is where the rubber hits the road for Smart Machines, as they finally get to have a direct influence on how a business operates and interacts with customers. Smart Machines can have different levels of autonomy when they act and influence results. Actions are very specific to a business domain. What are examples of such actions in real life? A tablet computer might provide a doctor with a recommended treatment for a patient's symptoms. A critical part of an aircraft could send a signal to the ground that it needs to be maintained once it lands at the destination airport. A mobile app might notify a taxi driver that a new passenger requires a ride. A bank could notify its customer that he or she has gone into overdraft. An insurance claim might be refused when it is suspected to be fraudulent. A message could be sent to a customer who has a high risk of churn to provide a special offer. A supermarket could order new supplies before it runs out of stock. A robot arm in a manufacturing plant might pick up a part that is no longer needed. A traffic sign could change the speed limit from forty-five miles per hour to thirty miles per hour due to a traffic disruption. And many more. These are only a few examples.

Five Phases for Action

The process of Smart Machines taking action can be separated into five different phases. In the first phase, the Smart Machine must identify a need for action. For example, perhaps a high risk of churn is noticed for a valuable customer, and an intervention is needed to keep the customer happy. In the second phase, the most suitable action is selected. This can be based on simple rules (e.g., "If temperature < five degrees, trigger action X")—in this case, we speak of automation. But it could also be a very complex decision that requires a Smart Machine to run algorithms, collate all possible options, and select the best one, relying on its previous experiences and the wisdom it has collected in its knowledge base. In the latter case, we speak of *autonomous actions* rather than automation.

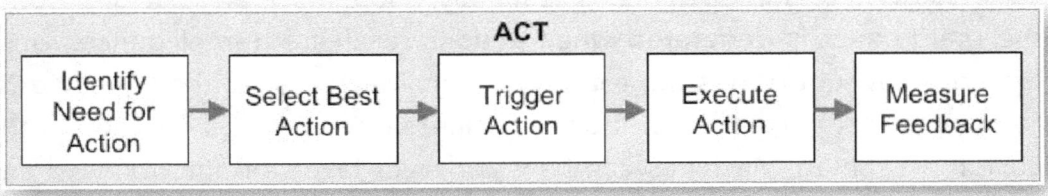

Figure 21: How Smart Machines Act

The third phase is when the selected action is triggered. This is comparable to the decision to execute a decision and the command to do so. The decision can be made by a human or a machine, depending on the application scenario. Only in the fourth phase is the action actually executed. Again, this can be done by the Smart Machine itself, another Smart Machine, or a human being. Finally, in the fifth phase, the feedback that resulted from the action is measured. This could be anything from a customer rating to a channel's sales conversion rate to an engine's sensor measurements.

The Levels of Autonomy and Action

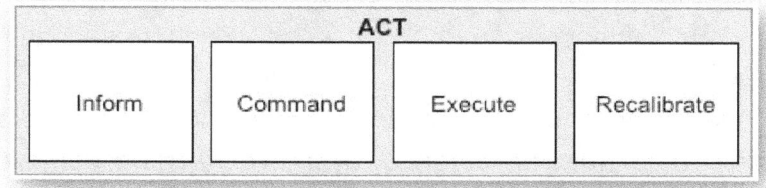

Figure 22: The Levels of Autonomy and Action of Smart Machines

Depending on the application scenario, a Smart Machine can have different levels of autonomy.

Level 1: Inform
In the first level of autonomy, the Smart Machine provides information to a human decision maker or another Smart Machine, which then makes a decision. The Smart Machine itself does not make the decision. The information can be general information (e.g., a map of a certain geographical area) or specific information (e.g., a particular route suggestion).

Level 2: Command
The second level of autonomy gives a Smart Machine the ability to select the action that has to be executed by another Smart Machine or a human

being. The Smart Machine is the decision maker but does not execute the action (e.g., the machine makes a decision to order more stock, which then is executed by a staff member in the store).

★ According to Gartner, by 2018 more than three million workers globally will be supervised by a "roboboss."[34] By 2020 autonomous software agents outside of human control will participate in 5 percent of all economic transactions.[35]

Level 3: Execute

The third level of autonomy includes the execution of an action directly by the Smart Machine. For instance, a Smart Machine can place a new order in the purchasing system, or a it can drive a car into a free parking space. In some cases a human decision maker has to actively decide that the Smart Machine should take over (e.g., by pressing the parking button in the car). In other cases, the Smart Machine can execute the action it chooses independently, but it can be overridden by a human being or another Smart Machine, like in the case of autonomous driving. In the extreme case, the Smart Machine is fully in control and cannot be stopped by a human, thus preventing human error—for example, the driver airbag goes off in case of an accident.

Level 4: Recalibrate

The fourth level of autonomy gives Smart Machines the ability to recalibrate their goals based on the measured results of an action. The Smart Machine does not simply follow a direction set by a human; it actually decides how to better reach a target (e.g., over 90 percent customer satisfaction under a given budget) by setting its own goals. For instance, the Smart Machine might realize that selling particular types of products in an online shop reduces customer satisfaction. Hence, it readjusts its goals and focuses on other types of products.

In Practice: "Robocars" are becoming a reality

Google's self-driving car is showing the way toward a future where vehicles can be operated without human intervention. These "robocars" are a good example of fully autonomous Smart Machines that are able to sense all relevant information on road conditions, traffic situation, and speed in order to think and calculate relevant movements and to act fully autonomously in adjusting direction and speed. There is still a long way to go to realize the vision of self-driving vehicles, but many carmakers are making big steps toward autonomous driving. For example, Tesla's autopilot mode allows the driver to take the feet from the pedals and the hand from the steering wheel. However, the autopilot mode is only a driver assistance system, as it functions best on motorways where it can expect pretty stable conditions of speed and car distances. The first accident reported by Google's self-driving car was on February 14, 2016, and it revealed another complexity of autonomous driving. The vehicle was driving in autonomous mode and had pulled to the right lane to prepare for a right turn. The car then sensed two sandbags blocking its way, and it came to a stop. After a couple of cars passed the Google car, it pulled to the middle lane, expecting that the bus coming from behind would slow down and let the car into the flow of traffic. That was not the case, and so the car crashed into the bus at slow speed. Such traffic situations are a normal part of driving. Every human driver is constantly predicting the movements of the drivers around him. Google's self-driving car made a wrong judgment that the human driver would give it space to change lanes. Humans are sometimes a bit more unpredictable than the standard algorithm, and Google will certainly expand the room for error in case of a human judgment next time. In the future self-driving cars will also be able to communicate with each other and prevent situations like these. However, as long as humans are part of the game, Smart Machines must always take the human factor into consideration.

Matching Capabilities to Business Needs

We have outlined the key forces driving the development of Smart Machines toward more sophisticated cognitive capabilities. Marketing leaders need to understand these capabilities in order to apply Smart Machines to real business needs. Furthermore, marketing organizations need to understand how to implement Smart Machines, develop the right algorithms, and enable machine learning. This requires new skills, new processes, and new partnerships, which cannot be built up by most companies over night. Companies need to embark on their Smart Machine journey by focusing on what matters most: improving the experience and value for their customers. How to get there is what we cover in the third and final part of this book.

Part III

* * *

The Transformation Journey

Chapter 8

Getting Your Marketing Ready

The future belongs to those who prepare for it today.

—Malcolm X

We Know Smart Machines Are Coming, But What Should We Do Now?

Many companies have made significant efforts to become more digital and connected in recent years. As the number of digital touch points with customers, partners, and things (IoT) has grown significantly, companies are challenged by the exponential growth of data that they need to analyze and process. Marketing organizations are at the center of that development, as they need to orchestrate the engagement and experience around the customer and create value for the customer. Therefore, the last part of the book focuses on how marketing leaders need to prepare and transform the marketing function around the customer experience, data, talent, skills, and the capabilities of Smart Machines on the way toward the algorithmic economy. There are three key areas for marketing leaders to invest in to prepare their organization for Smart Machines: (1) an omnichannel customer experience, (2) a harmonized customer data foundation, and (3) customer analytics, data science, and algorithms.

Invest in Omnichannel Customer Experience

Put the Customer into the Center of Your Marketing Transformation

Business models in the algorithmic economy are diverse and often very complex. The key element of any business model is to always put the customer journey into the center. We described in the first chapter how sensors are making the physical and virtual worlds increasingly intertwined; how Smart Machines allow us to generate, process, and analyze large amounts of digital data intelligently and context specifically; and how they are becoming more and more integrated into our lives. Smart Machines are revolutionizing the way you can interact and engage with your customers. The more digitally savvy your customers become, the more they will demand that you provide them the experience they've come to know from companies like Google, Apple, and Amazon. Many believe that this will put a lot of pressure on established players in traditional industries.

★ Smart Machine marketing requires to you rethink your entire business model and how you interact with your customers.

This is not about simply building a new digital channel—for example, a new mobile app. Customers will increasingly expect that you engage with them on their terms. In their book *Leading Digital*, George Westermann, Didier Bonnet, and Andrew McAfee recognize that "digital mastery goes well beyond websites and mobile apps to truly transform the customer experience and how you steer customers effortlessly through it."[36] Any Smart Machine transformation should therefore start with redesigning the customer experience.

Key Steps to a Revolutionized Customer Experience

Today companies like Macy's and Starbucks have chosen an alternative, more successful approach to business management that is customer-centric, focusing on the outstanding experience of each individual customer and on increased customer intimacy. The question is, what are the key elements needed to systematically create a more compelling customer experience in a digital world?

First, it's about listening to the voice of your customers. This requires gathering, integrating, and analyzing data about your customers from all customer touch points and from social media, along with finding new sources of external data. An outside-in view is created from many data points that indicate how the customer perceives the service in the whole context around service consumption. In other words, you try to see the world through your customers' eyes and listen to the customer voice. Digitizing the customer experience requires a trusting relationship with your customers, as they often need to share a lot of personal and sensitive data and information with you. In the future, many customers will decide whether they will do business with you or not depending on whether they feel they can trust you with their data.

Second, it is about using digital technologies to rethink and redesign the business processes that affect your customer. The key is to understand how the customer would like to interact with your company and your products and services. Sometimes this involves convincing and educating your customers about new digital technologies that can make their lives more convenient, better, or simply nicer. Starbucks's mobile payments and Macy's augmented-reality-enhanced fitting rooms are two great examples of this (both case studies are discussed in chapter 9). Customers are expecting a more personalized interaction in marketing, sales, and services, even if your business is very large, having millions of customers and operating call centers with thousands of call agents. Customers want to engage with you meaningfully via their preferred channels online and offline and be rewarded for sharing data about themselves. Social media is a two-way street. Customers expressing a complaint about one of your products or services on your company's Facebook page or Twitter handle are looking for a timely and respectful response that will take care of the problem.

The challenge is to provide a seamless experience by fully integrating the physical/digital experience: for example, being physically in a brick-and-mortar store while surfing online or using a mobile app. Customers are increasingly expecting your company to know their online interactions when they enter a physical store so that you can better help them. These are the two essential components that can be implemented independently from each other. However, when combined together, their value multiplies. When you know your customer better, you can design a better customer experience. When you infuse the digital into the customer experience, you can know your customer better. In fact, it is a self-enforcing loop, which gives you an ever-increasing competitive advantage. We will now examine both elements in more detail.

Achieving a better understanding of your customers' needs and behaviors is the first very-important step toward a successful digital transformation. Learning about your customers is one thing, but then it is time to do something with the new insights and the digital technologies that are available to transform the customer experience. The aim of this chapter is to explore the key steps needed to achieve this. It starts with building a vision of your brand.

Build a Vision of Your Brand Experience

Your brand is not part of the business. It is your business.[37]

—Daryl Travis

Every brand offers a promise to its customers. When I buy a Porsche, I expect to get a fancy and fast car that drives as smooth as butter. What is your company's brand promise? What does your brand stand for? We talked about how you can listen to your customers' voice using digital technologies. Now it is time to use these capabilities to understand how your customers perceive your brand today. What feelings do your customers have about your brand? Are they still interested in your brand promise? Maybe you need to change what your brand stands for to make it more relevant to your customers. Do your customers still believe in your company's brand promise? "When a brand is not true to what it promises, you know it. You feel it more than you think it," says brand management expert Daryl Travis.[38]

★ **The brand is not a communication strategy. It is what the customer feels, sees, and perceives.**

How can you make the brand promise a reality? Westermann, Bonnet, and McAffee observe that "many companies start by reenvisioning the way they interact with customers. They want to make themselves easier to work with, and they want to be smarter in how they sell to (and service) customers."[39] Smart Machines can help your brand to deliver what it promises. By creating a more compelling experience, you will change how customers perceive your brand.

Use Customer Journeys to Redesign Brand Experience

To redesign your brand experience, one method is particularly useful: mapping the journey of your customer. So what exactly is a customer journey? In a *Harvard Business Review* article, Adam Richardson gives the following definition: "A customer journey map is a very simple idea: a diagram that illustrates the steps your customer(s) go through in engaging with your company, whether it be a product, an online experience, retail experience, or a service, or any combination. The more touch points you have, the more complicated—but necessary—such a map becomes."[40] Designing customer journeys is a great tool to imagine and rethink how your customers experience your business in the algorithmic economy.

Think of a canvas. A customer journey map usually shows the journey of your customer on the horizontal axis, demonstrating typical moments of engagement and touch points with your customer or customer activities. For instance, it can follow the typical sales path from awareness, favorability, consideration, intent to purchase, and conversion to the out-of-box experience that is used by e-commerce marketers. It can also look at the customer journey after the product is sold to improve the after-sales experience. If your company is an insurance company that has a lifelong relationship with a customer, it might make sense to look at a typical day, week, or month of that customer to identify the touch points and how they integrate into daily life.

To ensure that the customer journey works for different types of customers, so-called "personas" are developed, which are fictive customers that you come up with for each of your customer segments. So first take a look at your customer segmentation. Then think of a fictive person who could represent the segment well. Each persona should have a name, city, age, educational background, professional background, lifestyle, living situation (e.g., married with kids), and other attributes that could be of interest in characterizing your segments. If your company is a bank, you might develop a persona like the following: "Benjamin Jackson is thirty-two years old and holds a bachelor's degree in biology from Princeton. He has worked for a pharmaceutical company in London as a research scientist. He loves playing soccer and playing the electric guitar. Currently he is saving up money to buy a small house in London, as he has just gotten married to his longtime girlfriend and they plan to have kids."

On the vertical axis, a number of different things can be noted for each step of the customer journey. This can include a description of actions, motivations, questions, and barriers that the customer experiences.

Moreover, it can contain the current touch points that the customer has with your company during each step and how these could be improved or replaced with new digital technologies. Some customer journeys even highlight the complexity that the change would entail. Finally, the last line on the axis could be what the digital innovation changes for each step would bring to the customer and to the business in terms of value. Not all digital innovations during the customer journey are necessarily the right ones to implement.

Make the Digital and Physical Worlds Seamless for Your Customers

The digital and real worlds are merging. Customers get messages from and interact with your company on a multiplicity of channels: traditional physical branches, online shops, mobile, direct mail, phone, TV, e-mail, chat, web marketing, social networks, blogs, and tweets, just to name a few. Shifting customer touch points and rising expectations for a better experience put pressure on marketing divisions to reinvent themselves. Westermann, Bonnet, and McAffee emphasize that "customers do not separate their online experiences from their physical experiences. They see products and services as a whole; they search for objective advice and compare. They want to engage with brands that care, and they share feedback openly—good or bad."[41]

* Each 1 percent improvement in customer experience quality-as measured by Forrester's Customer Experience Index-results in an additional $15 to $175 million in annual revenues.[42]

Companies have to seamlessly mesh physical and digital experiences to meet the demands of their customers. Yet for many organizations, this is a massive challenge. Things happen in a physical branch location and online or on mobile phones as if they have nothing to do with each other. Companies too often work in silos. When you redesign the customer experience, make sure you are not replacing the old physical experience with the new digital experience but rather improving the old by complementing it with the new.

The next step to build a customer-centric, algorithmic company is to invest in the data foundation that can run sophisticated algorithms on top of it once it has been established.

Invest in a Harmonized Customer Data Foundation

To get closer to the customer, you first have to know who your customer is. Westermann, Bonnet, and McAffee, who have studied the success factors for digital transformation for many years, emphasize that digital masters "put customer data at the heart of the whole customer experience. They become more scientific, using metrics and analytics to inform the change—everything from understanding current usage of their products and services to segmenting the customer base and proactively offering personalized deals and designing predictive marketing campaigns."[43] Digital technologies can help to build a profile of each individual customer, which can then be used to analyze customer behaviors and preferences and as a foundation to personalize interactions. For instance, when a customer calls in to report a product problem, the call-center agent can look at the customer profile and provide personalized recommendations that take into account the customer's individual characteristics and situation. Building such a customer profile is not always simple, however. In fact, it is very often a considerable challenge for many companies. Here are a few best practices that might help.

The Customer Data Ecosystem
We are confronted by the data explosion every day. We tweet, post, like, share, download, and upload all the time. As the number and capabilities

of digital devices soar and prices plummet, sensors and smart devices are digitizing a lot of our world that was previously not "readable" by any machine. This trend is accelerating further given Moore's law, which says that the processing power and storage capacity of computer chips double or their prices halve roughly every eighteen months. In addition, more and more people are able to buy and use mobile phones and smart devices around the world.

Despite more digital footprints, marketers still face the same challenge of how to capture information on their prospects or customers. If customers are sharing information on your products on Facebook, then that data is owned by Facebook and you need to ask for access to that data. Facebook might give you a share of that data based on the money you spend on Facebook ads (negotiation power) or the money you are willing to pay to Facebook. The new battleground is therefore focused on who owns the data and the most of the customer relationship.

Data can be distinguished into first-, second-, and third-party data. *First-party data* is your own data. This can include POS (point of sale) data, data from your owned media (website, mobile app, etc.), CRM data, and data from IoT devices (connected car, smart home, wearable technology, etc.). This data is collected from your own customers or audience, and you are in full control of what you capture. Therefore you can control the quality of the data, which makes it generally more valuable than data from the other two categories.

Third-party data is generated and captured in other forums, like social media platforms (e.g., Facebook) and IoT platforms (i.e., capturing behavioral and metabolic data), and can even be aggregated and enriched from multiple data sources. There is a big market to sell and buy third-party data to get better insight into audiences for personalized targeting by companies. In the past or predigital world, marketers bought those insights through research companies like Nielsen. Now the routes to buy and access third-party data are much broader and more numerous.

Second-party data is a fairly new concept that basically allows marketers to access first-party data. You can get the data directly from the source (i.e., publisher) or through a data management provider (DMP).

In order to capture most customer data, companies need to connect the different data sources, some of them outside their direct control. Therefore marketers need to build an ecosystem of data providers and partners to get more insight into their customers and audiences. Ecosystems also differ from area of interest (e.g., health and beauty versus sports) and regional differences based on local heroes, such as the social media platforms WeChat for China and LINE for Japan.

Identify Who Your Customers Are

First, we need to define the concept of *customer*. This sounds trivial, but in practice it often is not. Commonly, a company has more than one type of customer, such as the customer who does not pay directly for a product or service. End consumers are often the ultimate customers, but there are intermediaries like retailers who stand between and also form a group of customers. Think of Google's business model, which provides end users the service of providing web searches for free, but those end users generate value by viewing and clicking on ads. Companies that run AdWords campaigns and pay for the ads are also Google customers.

Potential customers might not be in your customer database yet but are also an important type of customer. In addition, business partners who help to sell your products might be a customer. If your customer is a business, it might make sense to create a hierarchy, especially when it is a large company with many subdivisions. Let's assume your customer is General Motors (GM) and you want to build a hierarchy. It might make sense, for instance, to divide GM further based on the type of products (e.g., automobiles, automobile parts, commercial vehicles, and financial services). Automobiles could have a further subcategory of GM's car brands (Chevrolet, Buick, GMC, Cadillac, Opel, etc.)

Customer centricity requires that you aim to create a compelling customer experience for all the different kinds of customers who are important to your business due to the value and different roles they play in your business model. The customer ecosystem is often very complex. Carefully defining each concept of customer and its role is a first stepping-stone to creating an improved customer experience. With every type of customer, your company already has some touch points. It might be the marketing or sales department; it could be services and maintenance. If possible, come up with a list and description of the touch points. The table below shows an example scenario of an electronic devices manufacturer. The customer type in this example is an end consumer that buys the product in a store.

Touch Point Description	Channels Used
Consumer gathers product information to make purchasing decision	Website
	Chat
Consumer compares prices and buys product online or in a store of a distribution partner	E-Shop (third party)
	Retail Store (third party)
Consumer registers product to extend warranty	Website
	Mobile App
	Call Center
Consumer uses the product and gets support or additional services	Website
	Mobile App
	Chat
	Call Center

Table 3: Customer Touch Points and Channels

Create a List of Things You Want to Know about Your Customer

Beginning to integrate and analyze data is not very effective when you haven't pinpointed exactly what you want to find out. Listening to the voice of your customer is an explorative process, and exploring always starts with questions. Start with a good set of questions about what you would like to learn about your customers. What are the things that interest you most about your customers from a business standpoint?

You can come up with an initial set of questions by yourself. Do not be afraid to ask the wrong questions. This is an iterative process. Once you find out more about your customers, you might want to adapt and refine your set of questions, and in this process you might come up with entirely new questions. It is even more powerful to come up with the initial set of questions in a brainstorming session with colleagues from different departments in your organization, as everyone is bringing another perspective, experience, and personality to the table.

So what might the questions be? This really depends on your business type, your customers, and the specific situation your business is in.

Some questions might be relevant for both business customers and consumers:

* How profitable is this customer for my business?
* Which products does this customer buy?
* What is the service-level quality this customer expects?
* Which new product would the customer like to purchase?
* Which new services could be of interest to the customer?
* What is the buying potential of the customer for my product?
* How likely is this customer to buy a complementary product?

Here are some examples that could be more specific to consumers:

* When does the customer come into the store?
* What is the income level and status of the customer?

* What is the profession of the customer?
* What is the age and gender of the customer?
* What kind of lifestyle does the customer adopt?
* Is this customer married?
* Does the customer have kids?
* Does the customer play any particular sport?
* Which movies does the customer like to watch?
* How much money does the customer spend with the competitor?
* Does weather have an impact on the customer's buying behavior?
* Do promotional activities impact this customer's behavior?
* Has the customer gone through any life-changing events recently (e.g., marriage)?

Other questions could be more specific to business customers:

* What is the financial performance of my customer?
* What is the planned spending budget of my customer?
* How much wallet share does my company achieve?
* Which relationships to the company do we own?
* Are there any contacts likely to be promoted to become executives?
* What are the biographies of the decision makers at the company?
* Are there any changes in leadership in this company?
* Is the company planning a corporate restructuring?
* Is the company undergoing any mergers or acquisitions?
* What are the strategic priorities of the company?
* What is the planned production output for this year?
* How does the company perform in comparison to its peers?

Integrate Relevant Data across the Enterprise and All Touch Points

Once you have defined the concept of "customer" for your business and identified a list of questions you would like to explore, it is time to integrate data that is relevant to understanding each important customer group. The questions you set up earlier can guide you here. Clearly, many questions cannot be directly answered by data that you can collect or integrate. But think of which data points can at least contribute to answering the questions, as sometimes there are workarounds. For instance, when you want to know the income level of your customer, the car model the customer owns might be a first indication—the owner of a Porsche Carrera is very likely to be of a higher income class than the owner of a Honda Accord. The data is usually distributed across your enterprise or even lies outside your company. Start with data that appears to be the most relevant to understanding your customers. Typically this is customer master data, such as name, gender, address, e-mail, phone number, date of birth, and other personal characteristics (like income, if available). When your customer is a business, it makes sense to store the company's details and structure but also the details of contact persons and decision makers.

Integrating data across organizational silos can be challenging. Many companies have several lines of business and have undergone mergers and acquisitions in the past. Often each line of business and even each department own their separate customer databases. It is not unusual that each sales channel (physical store, online, mobile, etc.) operates a separate set of customer data records. IT initiatives such as master data management, customer relationship management, and data warehousing have been initiated in many organizations to integrate data out of these silos, and some were probably more successful than others. Often resistance and politics between individual departments that do not want to lose control over their own customer data form a brick wall that needs to be overcome. From this you can add further internal and external data about the context of your customer.

Collect Additional Data from Social Media and the Internet

Social media and the Internet are very rich sources of information about businesses and consumers and should be exploited to better understand

and serve your customers. Social media platforms that allow users to create and share user-generated content are manyfold, as you can see in the table below.

Social Media Focus	Examples
Personal relationships	Facebook, Google+, Meetup, MySpace
Business relationships	LinkedIn, XING, Academia.edu
News, location, events, and opinion sharing	Twitter, TripAdvisor, Yelp, Foursquare, Eventful, del.icio.us
Photo sharing	Instagram, Picasa, Flickr, SnapChat, WeChat
Video sharing	YouTube, Vimeo, Periscope
Blogs	WordPress, Blogger, Blogspot, Tumblr
Boards and forums	WarriorForum, DigitalPoint, Nairaland, MineCraftForum, AVSForum, India-Forums
Online dating	Match.com, Plenty of Fish, Tinder
Knowledge sharing	Wikipedia

Table 4: Social Media Platforms

But how can you get access to the wealth of data created in social media? Blogs, boards, forums, Wikipedia, weather forecasting services, and news websites (such as those from *Bloomberg Businessweek* and the *New York Times*) that are open to the public can oftentimes be crawled by software tools, and hence many companies write scripts to collect this data. Alternatively, you can pay companies for this service. For instance, BoardReader is a service that very effectively searches the "human to human" discussions that exist on the Internet and captures the information. On some platforms that put a higher priority on the privacy of their users, the data is completely protected from the public and invisible to you as a company (e.g., some of the more serious online dating companies do not sell personal data).

For most other social media sources, access to data depends on the platform and on the privacy laws in your country. In the United States, a lot of social media data can be bought from so-called "data brokers" such as Gnip and Acxiom. The Federal Trade Commission (FTC) defines data brokers as "companies that collect information, including personal information about consumers, from a wide variety of sources for the purpose of reselling such information to their customers for various purposes, including verifying an individual's identity, differentiating records, marketing products, and preventing financial fraud."[44] For example, data broker Gnip offers, among other things, complete access to Twitter, Tumblr, Foursquare, and WordPress and managed public API access to Facebook, Google+, del.icio.us, Flickr, Instagram, Vimeo, and YouTube. Data broker Acxiom has around three thousand data segments for nearly every consumer in America, and data broker Datalogix, which gets data directly from Facebook, has personal data about almost every US household.

Be cautious. Even if the law in your country allows you to acquire and use personal data about your customers from third parties, the practice can be perceived as unethical by your customers, which can be very damaging to your brand, your relationship with your customers, and your entire business model. Data ethics is an important strategic matter for any organization in the digital age.

A more respectful way to collect personal data is to get the information, including consent to use the data, directly from your customers. Facebook and LinkedIn profile data can be collected when you let your customers create a link to their account on your web page or in your app. Many users are willing to share their data with you when they trust your company and understand the benefits of sharing data. Engaging with your customers on social media and other channels is probably the most sustainable way to collect more insights about your customers.

Once you have a solid customer data foundation across channels in place, the real fun starts by utilizing the data for advanced analytics.

Invest in Customer Analytics, Data Science, and Algorithms

The aim of marketing is to know and understand the customer so well the product or service fits him and sells itself.

—PETER DRUCKER

Three Types of Analytics: Descriptive, Predictive, Prescriptive

Business analytics applies advanced statistics and data-mining approaches for finding hidden insights and meaning in your data. Customer analytics applies analytics to optimize customer value. This can have a number of different goals. One aim could be, for example, to improve the customer experience in order to increase loyalty and prevent churn. Another aim could be to reduce costs per customer without reducing customer satisfaction. A third aim could be to make more revenue with one customer by getting the customer to spend a higher share of his wallet with your company. Business analytics can be divided into three main types of approaches: descriptive, predictive, and prescriptive analytics.

Descriptive analytics simply summarizes what happened. The most common type of analytics organizations use, it typically displays information within a report or dashboard view. Calculating key performance indicators and slicing and dicing within business intelligence software are typical approaches. Applications for descriptive customer analytics could be, for instance:

* the number of people who have visited my website by geography;
* the percentage of people who abandoned a filled basket in my e-shop;

* average demographics of my customers;
* variance of revenues within a customer segment;
* sales revenue and profitability by geography;
* customers who like similar products; and
* customers who react to similar promotions.

Predictive analytics studies recent and historical data to make predictions about the future or predict data we do not know but others might know. For instance, although *I* know my salary, that does not mean that *you* know it. You would need to "predict" this data. Predictive analytics uses various statistical, modeling, data-mining, and machine-learning techniques to achieve that goal. Example applications of predictive customer analytics include

* predicting each individual's response to campaigns based on interaction history and explicit rejections in the past;
* predicting sales customer demand, sales volume, and sales revenue;
* predicting which customers are most likely to churn;
* understanding impact and providing forecasting of cross-category promotions for key metrics such as units, sales, basket size, profitability, and store traffic; and
* forecasting buying habits and lifestyle preferences.

Prescriptive analytics uses the insights from the predictive analysis to "prescribe" an optimal action to the business decision maker. It uses optimization and simulation to ask, "What should we do?" Applications for prescriptive customer analytics include, for example, the following elements:

* optimizing product assortments and facings
* quantifying relationships between cross-channel prices and demand to optimize cross-channel prices

* recommending offers to generate the most effective personalized ads
* recommending products to maximize cross- and upselling

Customer analytics is your tool to get specific answers to the questions you pose about your customers. Want to know why customer demand is varying? Use predictive analytics to discover whether it might be due to weather, the economic situation, or personal factors. Want to understand where your most profitable customers are? Run descriptive analytics to calculate the profitability of your product by geography. Want to create a compelling new product offering? Predict buying habits and lifestyle preferences and optimize the price to make the new product entry a grand success.

Build Analytics-Driven Customer Profiles and Segmentations

A customer profile is a set of data points that characterize your customer. It can be used to build market segments so that each is treated differently in your marketing strategy. These profiles enable you to create advertisements, products, and services customized to each segment and to focus on the segments that are most profitable. A good customer profile and segmentation take the specifics of your business model and the relevant characteristics of your customers into account. We have shown you how to create a list of things you want to know about your customer. The questions you came up with can now be used to guide you in building your customer profiles and segmentations with the mountains of data that you hold about your customer and customer interactions.

Customer segmentation has been there for a while as a marketing strategy. However, the main ways of carrying out original research to obtain data used to involve face-to-face interviewing, telephone, mail, e-mail, web surveys, and focus groups. This, of course, only covered a small sample of your customer base, and the amount of data you could use was very limited. The customer profile and segmentation you can build today is based on a very rich set of internal and external data sources (mountains of data that your company has collected and integrated), and this gives way to nearly endless new possibilities to engage with your customers.

According to David Loshin and Abbie Reifer,[45] there are three types of customer data that can be used to create customer profiles: *demographic data* (such as age, gender, ethnicity, country of origin, race, marital status, education level, income level, dwelling type, number of adults in a household, number of children in a household, and/or number of cars owned), *psychographic attributes* (associated with personality, opinions, beliefs, interests, lifestyle, and likes and dislikes), and *behavioral attributes* (like product usage patterns, purchasing frequency, purchasing volume, and/or purchasing certain products together). Based on the profile information, customers can then be segmented. Loshin and Reifer emphasize that customer segments become more interesting when they are based on a combination of demographic, psychographic, and behavioral attributes.

To segment customers, often-complex algorithms are applied to the data: for example, clustering algorithms such as k-means, statistical mixture models such as latent class analysis, and ensemble approaches such as random forests. Yet the algorithms alone need to be supplemented with business domain knowledge. Applying different types of business analytics and data mining on top of the data-rich customer profile and segmentation can unlock value from the data.

Put Customer Data into Context and Filter Out the Noise

Have you ever bought an item online as a gift for your friends? It is most likely that you got further related recommendations based on that product purchase. The system made an implicit assumption about your preferences and lifestyle, which may have infuriated you, as they have no connection to you. Since the personalization system does not recognize the context in which you bought the product, it made the wrong assumption. This is a common problem for many personalization engines, which too often only provide an inferred view of customer behavior based on purchasing information without putting it into context. The system should have eliminated the gift purchase from your behavior profile.

This example shows that the same customer makes different choices and prefers different products or brands depending on the context.[46] According to G. L. Lilien, P. Kordler, and S. K. Moorthy, "Customers vary in their decision-making rules because of the usage situation, the use of the good or service (for family, for gift, for self), and purchase situation (catalog sale, in-store shelf selection, salesperson-aided purchase)."[47] Context can be categorized into

* life events like a new job, marriage, birth of a child, retirement, etc.;
* present setting and environment, such as location, people and objects nearby, changes to the setting, date, season, temperature, etc.; and
* emotional status and present sentiment (euphoric, pessimistic, energetic, etc.).

In the past, companies were able to collect some of the contextual information but were not really able to connect multiple context categories and context history. Smart Machines and further digitized touch points will help exploit the knowledge of context by identifying complex buying patterns, recognizing customer sentiment in real time (i.e., tone analyzer), and providing adequate actions.

Furthermore, the example of the gift purchase emphasizes the need to not only understand the context but also to cut out information or "noise" that has little or no impact on increasing customer insight and prediction. Given the explosion of recognizable customer interactions, Smart Machines need to develop filter and "forget" capabilities.

Derive New Insights about Your Customers from Unstructured Data

A lot of data from social media, the Internet, and even inside your company provide information in an unstructured form, such as text, images, and videos. Content analytics is needed to derive structured data from unstructured content. Once you have derived structured data out of the unstructured information, you can integrate that data into your normal databases.

Unstructured text can be, for example, a post on Twitter ("I loved watching the new *School of Rock* musical on Broadway #broadway #musical #awesome"). For a computer, this is a lot of gibberish. But text analytics, also known as "natural language processing," can transform this little piece of text into a format that is more understandable to a machine. This includes

* *lexical analysis* to study word-frequency distributions (for instance, the number of tweets that contain the words *"School of Rock"* and "Broadway");
* *syntactic parsing* and other types of linguistic analysis to make sense of a sentence by looking at the grammar of the sentence (for instance, in our little tweet, "I" is the subject, "love" is the predicate, and *"School of Rock"* the object);
* *identification of associations and relationships* among entities (e.g., it could be derived from the text that *"School of Rock"* is a Broadway musical); and
* *sentiment analytics* to specifically examine if the text expresses a positive, neutral, or negative sentiment (e.g., the word "love" signals a positive sentiment toward the musical).

There are many other advanced statistical and nonstatistical methods that computers can use to make sense out of a lot of text. A more advanced form of analytics is the recognition of images and videos. *Image analytics* and *video content analytics* allow you to automatically analyze the content of an image or video and derive structured information from it. If the picture or video shows somebody throwing a baseball in a stadium, the software would create keywords such as "baseball," "match," "stadium," "sports," and "lifestyle." A picture or video of a wedding could create the tags "wedding," "life-changing event," and potentially even the name of the people getting married using face recognition (as it is used by Facebook to identify friends in your photos). Images and videos can say an awful lot about who you are, what you like to do in your spare time, your lifestyle, and the friends who surround you. Again, we advise your company to be cautious and respectful here when applying these new technologies.

Apply Analytics to Understand Psychology and Transform the Customer Journey

For marketers, the question might be as simple as it has always been: "What do our customers desire, and what do they need?" Sounds very simple, doesn't it? Unfortunately, customers often desire things they don't need and need things they don't desire. In both instances, the customer experience and satisfaction might not last long. In order to build a profitable customer, it is important to sense the needs of the customer and shape the demand.

Customer journeys, as discussed previously, is a broadly used method aimed at gaining better insights, as the journey shows the end-to-end customer steps: inspire and search, inform and learn, choose and buy, use and consume, and serve and expand. In each step of the journey, the better companies sense and understand customer needs, trigger events, and moments of truth, the more likely they'll be able to convert a prospect into a customer or, in other words, increase the propensity of the customer to buy.

* **Customer needs**: foundation.
* **Trigger events**: change the course of the journey.

★ **Moments of truth**: highest impact on propensity to buy (cutting out the noise).

Customers are just human beings, and as humans they interact, reason, and decide very differently. The Merrill-Wilson breakdown differentiates among four personality types: *driver, expressive, amiable,* and *analytical*.[48] [49] In order to identify any personality, the model builds on two variables: (1) *Are people better at facts and data or relationships?* and (2) *Are they introverted or extroverted?*

★ **Driver**: Fact-based extrovert.
★ **Expressive**: Relationship extrovert.
★ **Amiable**: Relationship introvert.
★ **Analytical**: Fact-based introvert.

Most people will have a combination of major and minor types, which leads to multiple patterns. In a nutshell, customers will react very differently to the same message. Marketers have significantly improved their message effectiveness through better customer segmentation, which helps to optimize the outcome of the message, channel, and target group. To make it even more complex, it can also happen that the same customer will react very differently to the same message, perhaps due to a personal negative situation or life event.

Experienced sellers know their customers and are able to respond to different sentiments and adjust to diverse personalities. Machines can help marketers, sellers, and customer-facing personnel to maximize every customer interaction. Smart Machines will enhance the skills of employees engaged in the customer journey by leveraging key customer and context data to advise on the best way to interact with the customer.

The Next Level of Marketing

Understanding the customer has always been part of marketing. But the days when you could easily reach a high percentage of your potential customers through a single media channel are long gone. Therefore marketing organizations require more insight on

* who the target customers are,
* what needs they have,
* how and where to engage them,
* what creates brand loyalty and brand stickiness,
* and the context their customers are in.

Some companies might have a long way to go, while others are already pretty serious about redefining customer insight and customer experiences. The next chapter highlights some of the leading practices and companies as a source of learning and inspiration.

Chapter 9

• • •

Innovators that Can Inspire You

The United States is definitely ahead in culture of innovation. If someone wants to accomplish great things, there is no better place than the United States.

—ELON MUSK

It is too early to discuss transformations into the algorithmic economy, since Smart Machines are only beginning to enter traditional businesses. Hence, in this chapter, we would like to have a look at some successful marketing transformations and innovations in the last few years. You cannot copy these examples on a one-to-one basis, since the discipline of marketing is constantly evolving, and what was true yesterday might be out of date tomorrow. Nevertheless, these case studies can be an inspiration for your own organization. We can observe certain patterns of how complex transformations based on new digital technologies can work, but success requires much more than just the technological side of it.

Macy's Reinvents Fashion Shopping[50] [51] [52] [53]

Macy's, Inc. is an American retail icon headquartered in Cincinnati, Ohio. Its first store opened in 1858. Today it operates 786 department stores in the United States under the brands Macy's and Bloomingdale's. Its flagship store in Midtown Manhattan is a well-visited tourist attraction and landmark in New York City. With revenues of $27.9 billion in 2014, Macy's, Inc. is one of the largest fashion goods retailers in the world. The department store offers a range of products, including clothing and footwear, accessories, bedding and furniture, jewelry and beauty products, and housewares. *Fast Company* magazine named Macy's one of the ten most innovative retailers in the world. The three core business strategies today are what Macy's chairman and CEO Terry Lundgren calls MOM: My Macy's localization, omnichannel integration, and Magic Selling customer engagement.

My Macy's Localization

My Macy's localization focuses on localizing merchandise assortments by store location. Considering the number of branches and the size of the assortments, this creates a massive challenge for data analytics and operations. "We have redoubled our emphasis on precision in merchandise size, fit, fabric weight, style, and color preferences by store, market, and climate zone," commented CEO Terry Lundgren in an interview. "In addition, we are better understanding and serving the specific needs of multicultural consumers, who represent an increasingly large proportion of our customers."[54]

My Macy's Omnichannel Integration

The competitive advantage over pure online retailers like Amazon.com is that Macy's has its own physical stores. To make shopping more convenient,

Macy's offers customers the ability to buy an item online and pick it up in the store, and it is also able to ship goods from nearly all retail stores, turning them into highly efficient delivery centers with same-day delivery. Nearly all stores are also equipped with free Wi-Fi. Customers can do online shopping inside the stores using kiosks, reading through customer ratings and reviews, loading their own shopping list they've previously created online at home or on their mobile devices, and sharing information on products with friends on Facebook.

The RfiD tags on every item in the store create inventory visibility for the customer and allow automatic replenishment of the stock, which ensures that if something is available, the customer is also able to buy it. Interactive store directories enable visitors to find what they are seeking in the store. Macy's partners with Google to provide customers with instore maps to enable selfnavigation of its stores and offers tapand-go mobile payments via Google Wallet and PayPal using NFC (near field communication)–enabled Verifone card payment machines. "Smart" dressing rooms are another innovation that uses augmented reality, by which customers can use a wall-mounted tablet to view different colors and sizes or see customer reviews of an item.

My Macy's Magic Selling

Customer engagement includes interactions with customers not only in the physical stores but in all customer-facing environments, such as phone, live chat, and big-ticket delivery. This is achieved through tailored and real-time marketing, personalized customer service, and an optimized product mix. Macy's moved from sending out an abundance of generic e-mails to sending fewer but more targeted e-mails by gathering and analyzing data on customer reactions to different e-mail campaigns and levels of engagement. This could reduce subscription churn rate by about 20 percent.

Moreover, Macy's has added thousands of iBeacon devices to its 786 stores across the United States, a feature that is now available on the latest iPhones and some Android devices. These devices automatically open the retailer's mobile app and can send location-based coupons and offers to nearby smartphones using a low-energy Bluetooth signal. Customers get personalized advice and offers specific to their personal preferences and where they are in the store, taking into account what they have previously looked at online and on their mobile device before entering the store.

Starbucks Brews Digital Customer Experience[55 56 57 58 59 60 61 62]

You would think that selling coffee would be a pretty straightforward business, but Starbucks has made it an art and a unique experience. Founded in 1971, the company developed into one of the most recognized and respected brands in the world. By the end of 2013, Starbucks had 10,194 company-operated stores and 9,573 licensed stores in sixty-two countries. The company has increased profit and revenues for a number of consecutive years, with a total annual revenue of $14.9 billion in 2013. And within five years, Starbucks has turned from a technology laggard to a front-runner when it comes to digital customer experience. CEO Howard Schultz sets the expectations high: "We're not satisfied with the status quo. We want to continue to push for self-renewal and reinvention."[63]

My Starbucks Rewards Program

An important step has been the establishment of the very successful Starbucks loyalty card program. Introduced in 2009 to registered users of the Starbucks Card, it first offered incentives for users such as free Wi-Fi access, no charge for soy milk and flavored syrups, and free refills on brewed drip coffee or tea. Today the loyalty program has more than eight million US participants and many more around the world. Nearly one-quarter of all US transactions are made by My Starbucks Rewards loyalty members, and almost one-third of all US in-store transactions are prepaid. And the success of the loyalty program is not limited to the United States, according to CEO Schultz. "We are now seeing usage of My Starbucks Rewards at the same or even a higher rate than the United States in countries like China, Korea, and Canada, providing us with a significant sustainable competitive advantage over competitors in these markets."[64]

Mobile Payment Adoption on Large Scale and Customer Analytics

The original My Starbucks mobile app could locate the nearest store, and customers could learn more about the company's coffees and even build their own drink, but it did not handle payments. In 2009 Starbucks introduced its new mobile app for Starbucks loyalty card members, through which consumers access prepaid funds to purchase products at Starbucks. Starbucks brought pay-by-app to the large stage. In fact, 16 percent of US transactions at Starbucks take place via a mobile device—about seven million mobile payments per week. The new iPhone app allows customers to "shake to pay" and to tip digitally, as well as to earn free drinks and other perks. Curiously, Starbucks seems to be more successful in mobile payments than iPhone producer Apple has been, according to tech magazine *WIRED*: "Forget Apple Pay. The master of mobile payments is Starbucks."[65]

The loyalty card program and the mobile apps are creating an abundance of new data. Starbucks applies sophisticated analytics to decipher who you are based on the data. It has already profiled half of all loyalty card members.

Engaging Customers through Social Media and in Store

Starbucks has thirty-five million unique monthly digital visitors—comparable to that of a large media company—and is a leader in the social media world, with 94 percent of all Facebook users being either a Starbucks fan (thirty-eight million in total) or being friends with one. In addition, over seven million people are following Starbucks on Twitter.

Starbucks has created My Starbucks Idea, a customer community website where users can suggest new ideas to improve and innovate Starbucks's product and service offerings. Users can vote on which ideas should be selected and can follow the implementation of the idea on the "Idea in Action" blog. Starbucks has also launched Starbucks Digital Network, which allows customers to enjoy in-store premium digital content alongside their coffee. Customers can get access to a range of content, from the *New York Times* to the *Economist* and the *Wall Street Journal*, as well as other local content. Starbucks also has a dedicated team that is tasked with analyzing social media data. In 2014 Starbucks organized and presented a #HowWeMet portrait series on Starbucks Instagram, a global photo shoot. Users in eight countries were asked to capture images of people and their friends, colleagues, and significant others and describe how they met in Starbucks.

Digital Capabilities' Development and Leadership at Starbucks

In 2008 Starbucks created Starbucks Digital Ventures, an internal venture capital–style incubator for digital technology. To manage the digital transformation even more successfully, Starbucks created the position of the chief digital officer (CDO) in 2012. Starbucks's CDO, Adam Brotman, believes that a symbiotic relationship with IT is essential to success in digitally transforming the enterprise.

"We currently have one hundred projects active in IT, and thirty-five of them are customer- or partner-facing," commented former Starbucks CIO Curt Garner. He went on to describe how such project ideas were created and became reality. "We have a digital scrum that Adam and I chair between our teams, where we think through and whiteboard what are our next opportunities to create that magical experience for customers and for partners. Some of the great ideas we have come from outside our digital scrums. Adam and I had a chance to connect with a bunch of store managers recently, and talk with them about the type of interaction they're having with customers and they're having with partners and where they believe technology could reduce friction…we have tiger teams or SWAT teams that are assigned to specific projects and goals. We've been able to knock a lot of time and cycles off the work by having the thought leaders for digital and technology and their teams all together and working toward the same objective. Everything from the inception and brainstorming through the delivery is a jointly owned, team-focused, and very collaborative environment—something you might find more in terms of a smaller start-up and how they would approach the work than a multibillion-dollar multinational."[66]

How Nike Made Real Sports Digital

Nike, a $25 billion company headquartered in the Portland metropolitan area in Oregon, has become one of the front-runners for digital transformation. Here is the story of how this happened. "Most runners were running with music already," says Nike president and CEO Mark Parker. "We thought the real opportunity would come if we could combine music and data." So, as WIRED magazine reports it, "Parker picked up the phone and called a friend who worked at Apple, CEO Steve Jobs."[67] Hence the first digital service was created in collaboration with Apple. They developed the Nike+ Running app, an activity tracker that measures and records the distance and pace of a walk or run using the GPS built into Apple mobile devices. And it was a huge success. The products and services have become even more sophisticated over time. Today a small transmitter device is embedded in a pair of Nike shoes that takes the measurements and sends them to an Apple iPhone or iPod device.

Back in 2010 Nike invested in its own digital sport division, which employs engineers and scientists with previous experience at MIT and Apple.[68] The aim of the division is to develop devices and technologies that allow users to track their personal statistics in any sport in which they participate. The idea is not only to provide additional services and new products to customers; it is also about collecting tons of new data to better understand the customer and to make the interaction between Nike and its customers more meaningful. In 2012 another blockbuster product was thrown on the market: FuelBand, an electronic bracelet that measures the movements of its users throughout the day. "Nike has broken out of apparel and into tech, data, and services, which is so hard for any company to do," says Forrester Research analyst Sarah Rotman Epps.[69] In addition to the new products and services, Nike built a large number of new social sites dedicated to specific sports so that customers could share their successes and personal stories with one another and inspire others to use those new products and services. Mark McClusky from *WIRED* experienced it himself: "It's one thing if some company tells me that I'm slacking off, like when Nike+ sends an e-mail reminding me to get out and exercise. It's a whole different thing if people whose opinion I care about get on my case. Nike+ lets a user create a goal—one that other people can see."[70]

Samsung's Stepping-Stones to a Connected Life at Home[71]

We are about to see the biggest disruptions to our private lives in a long time. The concept of *connected things* stands for sensors and computing processors that are integrated with traditional products, interconnected with one another, and controlled through powerful software systems. What could you do if all your devices at home were interconnected?

Samsung, one of the largest and most innovative electronics manufacturers in the world, gives us the first glimpses of what is possible. Samsung, which is headquartered in South Korea's capital, Seoul, has put computing power and interconnectivity into many products in its product range. Tablet computers and smartphones can control and stream music, video clips, and photos on Samsung's smart TVs using Wi-Fi. Even the traditional household devices it produces (such as washing machines, fridges, ovens, and dishwashers) have a built-in processor and are interconnected with

Wi-Fi or Bluetooth connectivity. With an app on your phone, you can start the oven when you are still in your car. This gets even more interesting when you put NFC (near field communication) tags on different places in your apartment or home. You can program each NFC tag to perform a particular function when you put your smartphone on this tag. For example, your phone can automatically switch to the vibrate setting when you get into bed.

Samsung's vision goes well beyond this. In his keynote speech at the 2015 Consumer Electronics Show (CES) in Las Vegas, Samsung's chief executive, B. K. Yoon, announced that the company plans to invest more than $100 million to make everything Samsung produces interconnected via the Internet of things (IoT), from TVs and smartphones to fridges and washing machines. In the future, the entire home will be interconnected via Samsung's open IoT platform, SmartThings, which lets you monitor, control, and automate your home from wherever you are through a single mobile app.

Apple Watch–Can We Drive Behavior by Use of Personal Health Data?

As the Apple Watch was introduced, there was a big debate on the innovativeness and necessity of a device that is able to notify you about incoming messages, alerts, and some other events. But the watch's ability to capture all your daily movements—whether it be walking, running, standing, or sleeping—could influence your private and professional behaviors in many ways. With the right app, you can create your personal health profile, setting goals on calories, intensity of activities, and sleeping.

Many businesses and companies are already starting to monetize those capabilities. The data is used by insurers to understand how active you are and what is needed to support those healthy behaviors that will reduce the amount you pay for the insurance. Companies are using the data to support the health and safety of their employees. In the future, we may see that companies will incentivize their employees for getting at least seven hours of sleep every night or doing a number of workouts with a given intensity per week. Connecting daily behaviors based on health data, lifestyle data, and nutrition data will be the foundation of new businesses and incentives around customers, workers, teams, and societies. But this will also raise concerns about privacy rights. Regulations and policies around data privacy, good ethical practices, and legal responsibilities are needed to protect personal rights and minimize data abuses. Societies, represented by their political leaders, need to set the boundaries on balancing the risks and benefits.

Airbus Makes Your Luggage Fly Smarter[72]

Everyone knows that flying can be stressful. Arriving on time at the airport and checking in luggage is certainly not the most fun part of it. Reducing passengers' stress is the goal of the visionary project Smart Baggage by Airbus, in cooperation with IT provider T-Systems and premium suitcase manufacturer Rimowa. The center of this project is to design the first digitally enabled suitcase that can be controlled by a smartphone application. The target audience is frequent flyers.

This innovative suitcase integrates electronic tagging for paperless check-in and a scale to weigh contents. It is also equipped for real-time tracking and self-service drop-off at the airport. "At Airbus we care about innovation on the aircraft…we care about safety…and we also care about the overall experience," says Airbus's chief innovation officer, Yann Barbaux. "We need to think about the aircraft in its complete environment." The target location of the suitcase can be changed via an app, and it can even be delivered to a passenger's home or hotel door. The aim is to increase by 60 percent the likelihood that lost suitcases will be found again.[73] The benefits for passengers are evident. Additionally, it creates a great cost advantage for the airlines and transportation companies that are responsible for handling the luggage. Further services can be provided to travelers, such as dry cleaning and laundry services before the luggage is delivered to its final destination.

Vestas Uses Algorithms for Wind Energy[74]

Vestas Wind Systems, headquartered in Aarhus, Denmark, is the largest manufacturer, seller, installer, and servicer of wind turbines. Vestas has fifty thousand wind turbines in over seventy countries, with an installed capacity of fifty-one gigawatts. One would think that building wind turbines is mainly a hardware business. Yet these days Vesta's business model relies heavily on data, especially when it comes to choosing the right places to install a wind turbine. Wind turbines are a multimillion-dollar investment with a lifespan of twenty to thirty years. The location chosen to install and operate a turbine can greatly impact the amount of power generated by the unit, as well as it how long it is able to remain in operation. "Vestas turbines operate for decades, and clients demand to know how much energy they will produce and what their return on investment will be before they are installed," explains Lars Christian Christensen, vice-president of plant siting and forecasting, Vestas Technology R and D. According to Christensen, the cost of a mistake can be tremendous. "First of all, if the turbines do not perform as intended, we risk losing customers. Secondly, placing the turbines in the wrong location affects our warranty costs. Turbines are designed to operate under specific conditions and can break if they are operating outside of these parameters."[75]

Vestas realized that collecting data is key to its business success and started to invest in data innovation. "We needed to know where the goldmines of wind are hidden, and we needed to have more information to aid our decisions," says Christensen. "We quickly formed a project group that took the idea forward and set out some key performance indicators that had to be met in order to proceed to the stage where we are today." The company set out to create the most detailed wind libraries that ever existed for wind turbine purposes. For this purpose, Vestas combined and processed data from global weather systems with data collected from existing Vestas wind turbines around the world. The data included more than 178 parameters, such as temperature, barometric pressure, humidity, precipitation, wind direction, and wind velocity from the ground level up to three hundred feet, along with the company's own recorded historical data.

To process the masses of data, the Vestas Firestorm supercomputer was built, which has a capacity of around 2.8 petabytes and is one of the fastest supercomputers in the world. "We gather data from thirty-five thousand meteorological stations scattered around the world and from our own turbines," says Christensen. "That gives us a picture of the global flow scenario. Those models are then cobbled to smaller models for regional levels called mesoscale models. The mesoscale models are used to establish our huge wind library so we can pinpoint a specific location at a specific time of day and tell what the weather was like."[76] With computational fluid dynamic models using the data, the engineers at Vestas reduced the measurement grid that was originally 27 x 27 kilometers (about 17 x 17 miles) to a granularity 10 x 10 meters (32 x 32 feet) to establish the exact wind flow pattern at a particular location.

"We could pose the questions before, but our previous systems were not able to deliver the answers, or deliver the answers in the required time frame," says Christensen. "Now, if you give me the coordinates for your back yard, we can dive into our modeled wind libraries and provide you with precise data on the weather over the past eleven years, thereby predicting future weather and delivering power production prognosis. We have the ability to scan larger areas and determine more quickly our current turbine coverage geographically and see if there are spots we need to cover with a type of turbine. We can also assess information on how each turbine is operating and our potential risk at a site."

Vestas is a great example how a traditional manufacturing and industrial service company uses Smart Machines to radically improve its operations. The company was able to significantly improve accuracy of turbine placement and lower the cost to customers per kilowatt hour produced, thereby increasing customers' return on investment. What is surprising is that although computational power has been increased dramatically, the energy consumption can be lowered by as much as 40 percent. According to Christensen, the results have implications that go beyond the initial purpose of the project: "We can now answer these questions quickly to identify new markets for wind energy and help our clients meet aggressive renewable energy goals."

Preventing Fraud and Crime in Colombia[77]

Approximately $2.7 billion is laundered in Colombia each year.[78] Since a lot of money laundering is funneled through Colombia's banking system, the regulators require banks to find effective measures to identify money laundering. Grupo Bancolombia, Colombia's largest private bank, with more than six million customers and $31 billion in assets, wants to be a role model when it comes to regulatory compliance and takes this task very seriously.

A few years ago, the bank launched a number of money laundering analytic technologies and projects. Today it mines vast amounts of transactional data to find abnormal patterns and identify ongoing and potential money laundering or terrorism financing. Part of the focus was on detecting two particular money-laundering techniques often used by criminal organizations. The first type involves dividing a large transaction into smaller ones that fall below a statutory limit ($10,000 in the United States) and then having many agents deposit them into multiple banks. The second type involves fractionated transactions, which are large transactions that are scattered among several accounts. "Our objective was to replace traditional warning systems based on parameters and rules with data-mining models capable of detecting unusual or suspicious behavior through transactional data analysis,"[79] says Felipe Correa, compliance section manager.

The initiative turned out to be very successful. On one hand, the bank could reduce the number of transactions needing to be analyzed manually from twelve thousand to roughly six thousand a year, saving operational costs. "In the past, we needed over one thousand commercial team members to do the number of reviews we had to do. We now need twenty-two," says Ruiz. "We have been able to transfer almost 80 percent of those resources into bringing new business into the bank. These are enormous efficiency gains that are helping the company concentrate on improving the bottom line."[80] At the same time, the bank has increased the number of suspicious-operation reports it files with the government from four hundred to twelve hundred—an increase of 200 percent.

Touch and Travel Revolutionizes Public Transport Ticketing[81]

Imagine you could just press "Start Journey" in a mobile app to jump on a train and then click on "End Journey" to automatically process the payment once you reach your destination. You could use the same app to do this in any city where you are using public transportation—with no need to know which ticket and tariff, and how many zones you actually need; no standing in line for a ticket; no need to download and register for a new mobile app in each new city you visit. And the app would always choose the best price option for you, transforming your ticket into a day or even weekly pass by magic when you take the bus or subway several times a day. Would that not be awesome?

Touch and Travel makes this vision come true for public transport in twenty metropolitan areas and for all long-distance trains in Germany. It is an initiative run by Deutsche Bahn, Germany's largest railway provider, in collaboration with many local public transport companies. The mobile app is available on iOS and Android. Via the GPS (geolocation) of your mobile phone or via NFC (near field communication) touch points on the train or bus, your location is automatically determined when you start or end your journey. Once you start your journey, the app generates a QR code, which you can show to ticket inspectors or a bus driver asking to see your ticket. Travel has never been easier.

With this, customer expectations will be changing. Using public transport in a city that does not yet support Touch and Travel feels like going back to the Stone Age. We believe this case study is just a small taste of how mobility will be revolutionized in the future with digital services, data, and algorithms.

Why Uber Is Becoming the Biggest Fear for Taxi Companies-and What Might Happen to Your Industry

Many start-ups have recently brought disruption to the taxi business around the world. Take Hailo, for example, which offers an app to book a taxi wherever you are. Many taxi companies are not very enthusiastic about such new digital services, as they are losing control of the distribution channel and have to share revenues with another party. Things have become even worse for taxi companies since the Silicon Valley smash hit Uber started its global expansion. Founded in 2009, the service is available in fifty-three countries and more than two hundred cities.

The novelty of Uber is that the drivers are not conventional taxi drivers; rather, any qualified driver with an acceptable vehicle can provide the service. Offering a new distribution model via an app, Uber also completely replaces the delivery model that dominated traditional taxi operations. All hiring and payment is handled exclusively through Uber and not with the driver personally. Uber has developed algorithms that automatically adjust pricing to supply and demand.

USA Today named Uber the tech company of the year in 2013. However, there are ongoing protests from taxi drivers, taxi companies, and governments that believe it's an illegal taxicab operation. In Paris and London, taxi drivers even roadblocked the cities in protest against Uber.[82] France's interior minister has banned the service temporarily as a response to the protests in Paris. The protests are not very surprising, as the disruptions caused in the long-established taxi industry are enormous.

PYMNTS.com provides evidence of how Uber has impacted the pricing structures for taxi licenses in the large metropolitan areas of the United States: "Most major cities require a medallion license to operate a taxi or taxi company. Because the supply of medallions was low, the demand for those medallions caused prices to surge for decades. City regulators also cast a shadow on the industry by allowing prices to rise beyond their value for years. But thanks to the 'Uber effect,' these past two years paint a different picture for the taxi industry. According to the *New York Times*'s data, the price of individual taxi medallions in New York City dropped 23 percent in 2014, from $1.05 million to $805,000. Corporate medallions for companies traded at an average of $950,000, a 28 percent decrease from their peak."[83]

Disruptions Will Be the New Normal

The example of Uber shows that the new wave of digitization does not stop at the online channel. It includes every part of our lives through the new mobile channel, social media, and the Internet of things. It is not enough to simply set up a single project that looks at disruptive technologies to compete in this brave new world. Leading companies have started to rethink and question their entire business model. Those companies are also in the pole position to lead the next transformation around Smart Machines and algorithms, as they are built on digital and data. The next chapter focuses on the right setup, skills, and capabilities organizations need to be competitive in the algorithmic economy.

Chapter 10

• • •

The Pathway to the Algorithmic Economy

*If you're trying to achieve, there will be roadblocks.
I've had them; everybody has had them. But
obstacles don't have to stop you. If you run into
a wall, don't turn around and give up. Figure out
how to climb it, go through it, or work around it.*

—MICHAEL JORDAN

If you have witnessed a major organizational transformation before, you know what Michael Jordan is talking about. Although many people understand what needs to happen, making it happen is a different story. It requires a lot of "blood, sweat, and tears" and most of all perseverance. We believe that future marketing leaders need to be much closer to the customer and to the daily work that the organization is doing. In other words, leaders need to get more practical, or they will not be able to keep up with the speed of innovation. It is not about understanding every byte of data; it is about understanding the concepts, alternatives, and limitations to better coach and lead their staff. This chapter provides the key pillars for the adoption of Smart Machines in marketing and should help marketing leaders to develop their transformation road map along key principles around people, organization, processes, and technology.

Build the Capabilities for Smart Machine Marketing

Grow the Talent and Culture for the Algorithmic Business

Many new capabilities need to be developed in your organization during your transformation journey. The skills needed will depend on the industry you are in and your business strategy. You will need to decide which capabilities are differentiating and should be built in-house and which could be outsourced. We know for sure that data and algorithms will play a major role for the marketing department of the future.

The Key Skills for Programming and Maintaining Smart Machines

Programming and maintaining Smart Machines will be a key area where you need to develop fresh talent. An important skill set that needs to be grown in the algorithmic economy is what is commonly known as data science. Data scientists are specialists in processing raw data into features (that can be used for data models) and in creating and testing hypotheses to build new data models. A valid question is, are the skills of data scientists still needed in the same degree when a Smart Machine can also do the same activities? As a matter of fact, data scientists' role will be even more important in the future. Smart Machines are taught, not programmed. Data scientists are needed to write the algorithms that make a Smart Machine work and to maintain these algorithms.

The data science skills needed for Smart Machines are

* programming;
* data preparation;
* data engineering;
* statistical modeling;
* machine learning;
* artificial intelligence;
* business domain know-how;
* natural language processing; and
* image and speech recognition.

It is no secret that such skills are currently in very high demand, and it is hard to acquire data scientists on the market. Hence it becomes even more important to use the data scientists you have or to teach other people in your business the same skills, such as by developing a trainee program within your company for young university hires or existing employees that would like to move into a data science role.

Scaling Data Science Innovation

Many companies underestimate the talent they already have in their company and, even worse, don't understand how to tap into this pool of talent. We believe that it's time to rethink the way companies identify, develop, and cultivate skills and talent. Companies can, for example, apply the concept of "hackathons," which are quite famous in software development to identify talent for data and Smart Machines. Those events allow a very dense way to assess and identify potential candidates who might not have studied math or computer science but have a natural talent and passion for solving complex problems, an affinity for numbers, and the imagination to see patterns.

The next step for data science is to move from doing successful prototypes in a small silo to scaling them afterward to the entire business. A visible trend is the emerging industrialization of data science, which is underpinned by a number of developments. Vendors increasingly support the management of analytical models built by data scientists over their entire life cycle, when they are scaled from prototype to companywide adoption. So far, the management of analytical models has been rather disorganized in most companies. Data scientists would create new models on a use-case-by-use-case basis. Those models actually doing what they promised to do would be deployed in operations. An end-to-end management of the models and a reuse of solution patterns for analytical models across the enterprise have not been actively enforced or governed. In a new project, companies often start nearly from scratch, although a similar model might have already been developed in a different business unit.

From an organizational point of view, it makes sense to have a centralized data science unit that can support data scientists in decentralized business units. A central data science unit can ensure that learnings are incorporated and fed back to the organization and that analytical models are consistently governed, even after they are handed over to IT. Closely connected to this is the concept of the *model factory*. The idea is to bring automation and scalability to the process of building and deploying predictive models. To find the best models, a huge number of models are built and tested using software tools that provide a high degree of automation during development. At the end of the process, only the best few models are deployed.

Finally, from Gartner's Alexander Linden comes a thrilling concept called the *analytics marketplace*.[84] Some companies like Microsoft, RapidMiner, and FICO have created marketplaces where third parties provide data science services and additional functionality, which can be purchased by users of the analytics platforms. This can become a true game changer. Similar to the third-party apps and services provided at Salesforce.com, analytics marketplaces could become a source of millions of very domain-specific analytics microapplications that drive innovation.

Today we stand only at the beginning. We are convinced that in a few years' time, data science and advanced analytics will be as industrialized as traditional IT. What has changed with the rise of data science is the speed with which new applications are developed and deployed, the increased willingness to experiment, and the direct way data innovates business models and business operations. Now it needs to be scaled to the rest of the enterprise to reap the full benefits.

While centers of competence for analytics and data labs have served for building up data-driven skills and competencies within a company, we believe that this is not enough given the fast-path transformation toward the algorithmic economy. In particular, the challenge is to leverage existing data-science skills for real business transformation within the business departments. An interesting model for organizing your business in a more effective way comes from the agile world.

Self-Organization in Squads, Chapters, and Tribes

One of the innovative concepts to best leverage your talent is to take a tribe approach that is based on leveraging groups within a company and cultivate those tribal structures to drive new behaviors or skills into the company.[85] An early adopter of the organizational design was tech innovator Spotify and other growth companies. Recently some traditional companies started to adopt the model too, including global bank ING.[86]

> ★ A new organizational setup of tribes, squads, and chapters-invented in the agile community and used in tech start-ups and traditional organizations-helps companies to most effectively utilize and replicate the data science and digitization skills to innovate their business.

The most granular group in this concept is a *squad*. A squad has a clear long-term mission, a responsibility for a business product (e.g., a mobile app or an analytics model), consists of three to nine people, is colocated, and is able to provide end-to-end delivery for the mission it aims for. Each squad is led by a product owner, who has the final say in everything for the squad and represents the squad to the business. Squads are self-steering teams that consist of different skill sets and roles. Since they can focus on one particular mission for a long time, they can become real experts in their area.

For instance, at ING bank there is a squad for mortgage applications that is responsible for providing a user-friendly and efficient path from first mortgage request to final approval. A squad for search engines is responsible for developing the best and most effective search engine across all of ING's digital channels. In one squad, we can find people from marketing, product management, formula management, data analysis, user experience, and IT. The mix of people is determined by the mission of the squad.

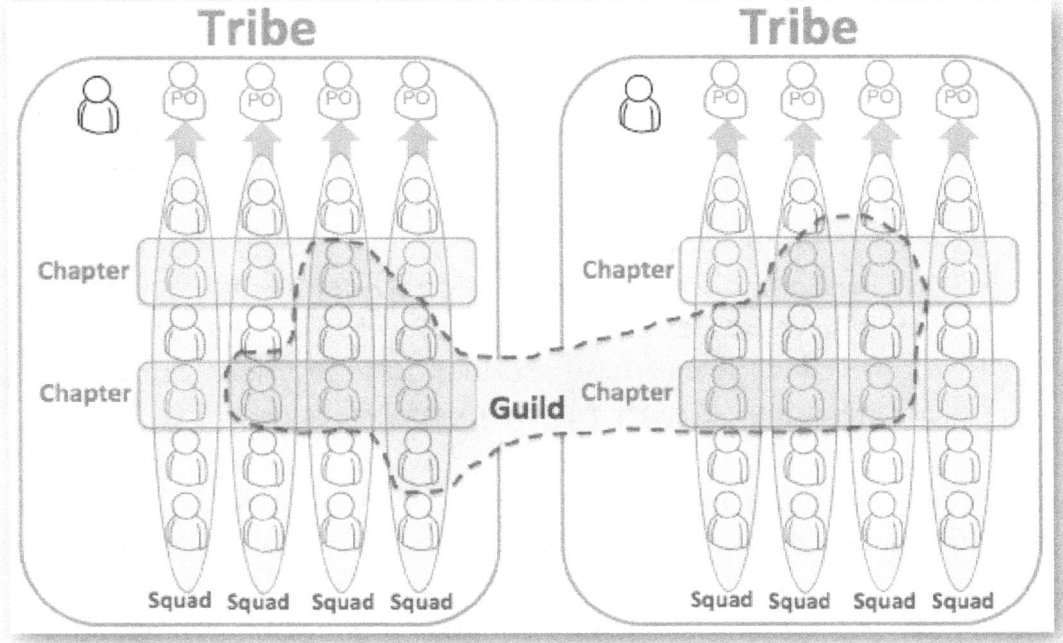

Figure 23: Tribes, Chapters, Squads, and Guilds (Source: Henrik Kniberg and Anders Ivarsson, "Scaling Agile @ Spotify with Tribes, Squads, Chapters & Guilds" (2012). http://blog.crisp.se/2012/11/14/henrikkniberg/scaling-agile-at-spotify)

Coordination between subject-matter experts across the squads happens in *chapters*. For instance, all software testers get together in one chapter, and all data scientists meet in another chapter. In a chapter, members work with other people with similar skills and competencies. This ensures that economies of scale are still realized through knowledge sharing and creation of tools and assets shared across tribes and squads. Each chapter has a chapter lead, who is the line lead for all the chapter members. The chapter lead is also responsible for the coordination within the chapter and with other chapters.

Several squads that have interconnected missions form a *tribe*. A tribe consists of fewer than a hundred people. A tribe leader makes sure that knowledge and insights are shared within the tribe, establishes priorities, allocates available budgets, and forms the interface with other tribes. Let us return now to our previous real-life example of ING bank. There one tribe is responsible for mortgage services, and another tribe is responsible for securities and private banking. There is also the role of the agile coach, who coaches individuals and squads on agile methods.

Last but not least, a *guild* is a more organic and wide-reaching community of interest across squads and tribes to share knowledge, tools, code, and practices.

★ This organizational model is not good for all business areas. It is, however, particularly strong in areas where you need a lot of new product development during digitalization and Smart Machine transformation.

The idea is that more and more employees want to follow those tribes or tribal leaders on the path to excellence. In that sense, tribal leadership is more a talent magnet than a prescribed organizational model where you deploy talent based on old-school controlling principles of head count, funding, and share of business growth. With the right talent and tribal leaders in place, companies can not only encourage internal talents but will also be able to lure external talents to move into that space. Tribal leaders should be the face of the company to demonstrate its ambitions and analytics capabilities at conferences, to professional networks, in media, and to universities.

With the introduction of such an organizational model in some parts of the organization, you will have other parts of the organization that will still stay in the traditional, waterfall-driven IT delivery model paradigm. This will create new challenges of synchronizing the two organizational approaches.

Run in Two Speeds with Bimodal IT for Digital Innovation

Gartner has suggested the adoption of a two-speed model for delivering IT projects for digital innovation. The key idea behind bimodal IT is that IT needs to offer a second mode in addition to traditional IT that is more risk taking, agile, and customer-centric in order to drive digital and analytics innovation more effectively.[87]

* *Mode 1* has a focus on reliability, is plan and approval driven, uses large-enterprise IT suppliers, and typically follows a waterfall approach for implementations.
* *Mode 2* emphasizes agility and hence uses agile implementation approaches. It often utilizes small, innovative new vendors and works closely with the business to drive fast and frequent customer-centric business innovations.

There are many organizations that have started to establish a second, more agile mode of IT (e.g., in the form of a data science lab, a digital factory, or an agile development and DevOps department). They usually run into two major challenges that impede them from reaping the expected benefits:

1. The two modes of IT are not synchronized well enough.
2. Business is not able to engage effectively with agile IT.

We will explain these issues in more depth, along with some ideas on how to resolve them.

Synchronizing the Two Speeds

What many organizations get wrong is that they focus too much on creating the new agile mode 2 of IT. However, this is only one component of implementing a bimodal IT. The real challenge is how to synchronize both modes so they can act as a team. Having them in silos will not only create conflicts but will also limit the success of any projects that need both mode 1 and mode 2 resources to succeed—which is usually the case. So what organizations need to establish is a bridge between the two modes.

Practically speaking, it all starts with mutual understanding and respect between the two modes. If mode 1 resources have the feeling they are a second class of IT, they will stop supporting mode 2 and hinder it wherever possible. Leadership needs to communicate that no mode is better than the other and that both modes of IT are equally needed for success. Mode 2 resources need to understand that mode 1 is crucial to renovate the core of IT, which enables innovative digital apps to be built on top of a healthy infrastructure efficiently and securely.

Moreover, there are touch points between mode 1 and mode 2 that require bimodal synchronization through explicit governance:

* When a new application is planned to be developed, selection criteria have to be defined that outline which implementation should be done in which mode of IT.
* When a new mode 2 implementation project is starting, it has to be examined to see if interfaces to mode 1 applications are needed and/or if other mode 1 resources are required.
* In particular, when the mode 2 product is supposed to be released in a mode 1 production environment, traditional release management needs to already be involved at the beginning of an agile project.
* Finally, when a mode 2 product is released, there might be a decision to further manage it in mode 1 in the future.

Business Needs to Become Two-Speed Too

Today's businesses are not ready yet to engage with mode 2 IT in a productive manner. There are two main reasons for this.

First, the second mode of IT is all about experimentation: trying out new features, new approaches to analyze data, and new ways to interact with customers, and taking into account that many of the experiments will not turn into viable products after all. Today most traditional organizations have not developed a mind-set for experimentation yet.

Second, using agile IT methods requires a much more intense participation of business during IT projects. Business is used to "throwing business requirements over the fence," where IT would gather those requirements, take a few months or even years to implement them, and then come back eventually for testing. In the meantime, the business doesn't need to spend much time on the IT project. This is not the case for agile projects. In each sprint, the business needs to closely work with the developers and define the business requirements "on the run" during the project.

These two points highlight some of the obstacles that come up when there is a two-speed organization on the IT side but only a one-speed organization on the business side. The solution is simple but substantial. Many large organizations that we work with have recognized the need to establish a second mode of business that is more experimental and fast paced and that enables real digital innovation.

The consequences are visible. There are more and more business labs and business innovation centers of large enterprises popping up around the world, in addition to data labs that work with agile IT to come up with and test new innovative ideas in a fast mode. They aim to imitate a start-up environment where creativity, experimentation, and disruptive innovation are in the focus. The results are impressive so far. Mode 2 IT can be much better utilized and the collaboration between business and a bimodal IT becomes significantly better when a two-speed business has been established.

This is only the beginning, but one new imperative clearly emerges. It is time for a two-speed business approach in any organization. The pace of change will become faster, and volatility will increase in the future.

In addition, the way organizations will consume IT in the future will be via cloud services.

Move Your Marketing to a Cloud Computing Environment

Many of the services and providers for Smart Machines will offer the full breadth of their offerings in the cloud and only a light version as an on-premise solution. The cloud offers a vast ecosystem of analytics solutions and algorithmic marketplaces using APIs. Moving some of the data and functionalities to the cloud will therefore be imperative for marketing departments.

★ Many algorithmic marketplaces and data services are only available in the cloud, and most digital marketing happens in the cloud, which makes it imperative to move a majority of your marketing functions there as well.

In layman's terms, cloud computing means that the computer hardware and software you use is located and managed in a centralized location somewhere else, and you do not have to worry about installing and maintaining it—you simply use it. An example of this is Amazon Web Services, which allows you to rent out computing power for whatever you need to process.

The Different Types of Cloud Environments

Clouds can be classified as public, private, or hybrid. In *public clouds*, the processing and storage of your data and of other companies' data can happen in the infrastructure, which is provided by a third party. The same server might first perform one task that your company has scheduled and then a task scheduled by a different company. In a *private cloud*, this cannot happen. Your data is stored and processed on computing machines that cannot be used by anyone but your company. Often the company is the owner of the infrastructure. A *hybrid cloud* is a combination of a public and a private cloud. It requires interoperability and portability of both applications and data to allow communication between the private and the public cloud.

★ Cloud computing can be private, public, or a hybrid of both.

When the cloud is managed by a third-party provider, another classification can be made with regard to the level of outsourcing:

* *Infrastructure as a service (IaaS)* just provides the physical computing environment.
* *Platform as a service (PaaS)* typically provides operating systems, programming language execution environments, database software, and web servers, in addition to the hardware.
* *Software as a service (SaaS)* manages and provides application software and databases on top of the platform.
* *Business process as a service (BPaaS)* includes everything mentioned previously, and in addition, the whole business process is outsourced to the cloud provider (often these business processes comprise customer care, administrative tasks, and business support).

Why Cloud Computing Can Create Advantages

Cloud computing provides an on-demand service for users, who do not have to worry about the infrastructure management behind that service. Many cloud environments use standardized access mechanisms, in contrast to the thousands of customized individual system interfaces that exist in today's enterprise data environments. A particular characteristic for cloud computing is that resources are pooled and are multitenant. In private clouds, all tenants are within the company, whereas in public clouds, other tenants can be external parties.

A strong benefit of cloud computing is its rapid elasticity. Usually the different tenants of a cloud system have computing consumption peaks at different times. This means that a cloud tenant in need of a lot of computing power at a particular moment can use all the computing power that is not used by other tenants at that same moment. This is typically much more computing power than would be available in a traditional environment, where resources are not pooled. Moreover, since cloud computing is provided as a service, the service can be standardized, and its performance can be measured, audited, and certified.

And finally, as already mentioned in the beginning, more and more functionality provided by marketing software providers will simply be cloud only, with no real on-premise alternative. A great example is the leading CRM software provider Salesforce.com, which is predominantly available as software as a service through the cloud.

Navigating through the Hurdles and Obstacles

Algorithmic Result Quality and the Need for Judgment

Using algorithms to make or automate decisions can create unwanted risks.[88] Algorithms might learn things from the data that simply are not true. This can happen because patterns discovered may not represent any underlying rule. Another reason for discovering things that do not represent reality might be that the model set may not reflect the relevant population and data may be at the wrong level of detail. Furthermore, algorithms might discover things with analytics that are true but not useful: for example, because they are already common knowledge or they cannot be used.

★ In a world in which many decisions are made by Smart Machines, assuring the quality of the algorithms is crucial to preventing damage. In addition to the management of analytics quality, addressing data quality issues with an enterprise data governance program will be essential to prevent constant damages.

When using Smart Machines for automating decisions, it is crucial to apply thorough judgment to check the outputs and actions of the Smart Machine by having human supervisors monitoring the operations in centralized control centers. A related problem is that analytical skills are concentrated in too few employees. So argue Shvetank Shah, Andrew Horne, and Jaime Capellá in an article in the *Harvard Business Review*: "'Informed skeptics'—the employees best equipped to make good decisions—effectively balance judgment and analysis, possess strong analytic skills, and listen to others' opinions but are willing to dissent. They're the kind of data-savvy workers every company should try to cultivate."[89]

And last but not least, data quality of corporate data sources will need to be managed with an effective enterprise data governance program. Algorithms can be only as good as the data that is provided to them.

Data Protection and Legal Barriers

In nearly all developed countries, there are high legal standards when it comes to using data that can be linked to natural persons. Since the legal framework differs country by country, it creates a huge barrier to companies that want to scale a Smart Machine application globally. Regulators are putting increasing pressure on companies to enforce data protection laws. In some countries, public media and nongovernment organizations investigate how data privacy is protected in commercial organizations, and any revelation can cause a cascade of negative press and a severe impact on brand reputation. In most cases, customer consent is needed if the data is going to be used beyond the original valid purpose of data collection and processing.

* Effective and efficient customer consent management across various countries and throughout all channels and applications will be a differentiating capability for Smart Machine marketing to enable agility and compliance.

A key capability for any company moving to Smart Machine marketing is to effectively standardize and simplify the way customers provide their consent, how data is processed, and how the consent information is stored and managed across the enterprise. A general rule is to provide customers as much detail as possible in a transparent and easy-to-understand way. Customers should have the option to opt in and out of different aspects of data usage and be able to adjust their privacy settings at any time without wasting too much time looking for where the options can be set. For large corporations, it makes sense to establish a central function that documents country by country how data protection laws need to be applied to create synergies.

Digital Ethics and Corporate Values

A key stepping-stone for your organization on the way to Smart Machine marketing is to find your strategic positioning regarding digital ethics that is in line with your corporate values. Laws only define the lower boundary of ethics—that is, "the red line." The corporate and brand values should define the positioning of your company with regard to digital ethics, which should be documented in the digital ethics charter. It has to consider customers' willingness to share personal data and be served by autonomous machines, and the sensitivity in how data is used, which can differ by age, personality, and especially by geography. Hence, the digital ethics charter should set the ground rules and take into account geographic and other types of nuances that should be specified and detailed.

* ★ Laws only define the lower boundary for digital ethics-that is, "the red line." The perception of morality in each country and the values connected to your brand are the actual drivers for defining a digital ethics charter.

Beyond this, Smart Machines raise a number of ethical questions when machines make autonomous decisions that actually need a moral judgment. An often-discussed theoretical example is the one of a self-driving car that encounters a child standing in the road. Should the car swerve in order to avoid the child, thus putting the driver at risk? Or should the car stay on its course, protecting the driver but possibly causing grave injury to the child? This might seem a bit constructed, but there are many other cases which actually did happen. For instance, in 2016, when Toyota's auto loan division had to pay back $21.9 million in restitution to thousands of black, Pacific Islander, and Asian customers who were charged higher interest rates than white borrowers based on an algorithm.[90]

Cultural Resistance and the Future of Human Labor

As much as people are fascinated by science fiction movies, many also fear that robots and AI will ultimately dominate our world. Is this just the ordinary human phobia surrounding new developments for which we are not able to see the end of the journey yet? What we can say today is that Smart Machines and robots may not take over our planet, but they will replace a significant amount of work that had previously been performed by humans. In their 2011 book *Race Against the Machine*, Erik Brynjolfsson and Andrew McAfee even predict that those jobs replaced by Smart Machines will not be offset by jobs created through this new technology.[91] However, we believe that new, as-yet-unimagined jobs and workplaces can offset some portion of "old" jobs destroyed. If societies have learned from the past, then we will see much more forward action than fights to preserve the past. Smart policies designed by global leaders in politics and business, for example, could suggest new job models that give us more personal time back when Smart Machines take over some of the tasks we used to perform ourselves.

Cybersecurity and Cyberterrorism

Cyberattacks on all kinds of private and public institutions have emerged into one of the biggest threats to our highly connected and digital world. Criminal networks and international terrorists are constantly improving their capabilities to identify and attack vulnerabilities in applications, net-works, devices, buildings, and factories. World-leading companies have been affected by data breaches, leading to a significant amount of sto-len customer and transactional data. From a marketing perspective, data breaches can destroy brand reputation and might even force companies out of business due to the loss of customer trust.

Therefore, companies and marketers need to understand the business risks associated with highly connected Smart Machines and the depth of data. This could also mean that under specific circumstances, marketers will make choices against applying sensitive data, as the risk to the brand outweighs the potential optimization benefits. We encourage CMOs and marketing leaders to establish data privacy and security roles and responsibilities within their marketing organizations. Moreover, this will also allow a faster reaction in case of cyberattacks and the initiation of countermeasures.

Customer and Social Acceptance

As with every economic transformation in the past, the move toward the algorithmic economy will lead to short-term repercussions. Smart Machines will have the capabilities to not only enhance human workplaces but oftentimes to replace human labor or even make whole jobs redundant. On the other hand, new jobs and new business will be created that leverage new capabilities around IoT, smart technologies, algorithms, and data. From a customer perspective, acceptance of new technologies or solutions is mostly linked to the value that is created for the customer. For example, customers value Smart Machines as call-center agents only if they help to solve problems quicker than their human counterparts. On the other hand, the social acceptance of smart agents might be lower, as many human jobs will be replaced by machine labor. However, economic progress was and always will be fueled by increasing the value for customers and will therefore drive their willingness to pay for the added value. This should be the key principle for companies while applying Smart Machines.

Five Steps to Start Your Smart Machine Transformation Today

We hope you have enjoyed reading this book. Our intention is to inspire you with the art of the possible, give you an understanding of the technologies behind Smart Machines, and to show ways you can prepare your organization for the future. If this all sounds fine to you, but you are overwhelmed and paralyzed by the complexity of the topic, here's a brief recipe for how you can start your own Smart Machine transformation journey today in a few simple steps.

1. Create a Sense of Urgency within Your Organization

Every journey starts with a first step. For companies, this means creating a sense of urgency and an understanding within the organization of how Smart Machines will change individual lives, workplaces, processes, organizations, businesses, economies, and societies. Marketing needs to play a leading role in driving a positive and productive mind-set of how Smart Machines will change the world around us. See yourself as an evangelist in your organization, promoting the changes that are to come and the urgency to act.

2. Find Partners and Allies within Your Organization

You cannot do it alone. Find supporters and partners who share the same beliefs and vision as you. Remember that the transformation is happening across all functions and business units. You'll need allies in IT, sales, services, production, HR, finance, and so on. Decision makers, perhaps even outside the marketing department (e.g., in production or product development), will help you make a co-investment in the core technologies needed for an algorithmic business. Partners will also help you to discuss, challenge, iterate, and adjust the journey. Always remember that the transformation is happening across all areas of business life and will affect every individual professional. People will listen to you!

3. Analyze Business Potential and Establish a Common Vision

As a third step, marketing managers should aim to understand the implications of Smart Machines for marketing in their industry and for their company and to create a common understanding across the enterprise. In particular, areas of high value and some of the sweet spots and quick wins for your organization should be identified. This can serve as input to jointly create a vision with your partners and allies that you can present to your management board. Besides developing a vision, it will help to define design principles and key underlying capabilities that will help you and your partners to make the right choices.

4. Identify Low-Hanging Fruits and Run First Projects

The best way to start practically is to apply Smart Machines in a small defined scope and to experiment with the technology for a real-use case that offers a quick win. This allows your organization to build up a practical understanding of the technologies.

One example for getting started with Smart Machines is behavioral targeting, where you leverage cognitive machine capabilities to analyze customer conversations from e-mail, messages, call centers, and social media to understand audience patterns and personalities. New or enriched insights could then be used for improving impressions and click rates by personalizing e-mail content and offers. As many companies already have experience in e-mail segmentation and targeting, you can compare Smart Machine–infused campaigns with traditional data-driven campaigns.

5. Communicate First Successes and Expand the Scope

To keep partners, stakeholders, executives, and employees engaged, it is important to show and celebrate successes, even small ones, as they are important steps in getting closer to the vision. Communicate what you learned from facing brick walls or what you changed to overcome them. Given the pace of innovation, the more companies are able to share knowledge, experiences, and learnings, the faster these companies will be able to establish Smart Machines and innovate their business models. Then expand and scale successful cases as fast as possible to support cases based on similar patterns. This will also help you solve the capacity gap on Smart Machine talent.

Now Go and Start Your Transformation Journey

Without a shadow of a doubt, Smart Machines that autonomously sense, think, learn, and act will make a profound difference to your industry and to the way marketing and sales will find success. The change process will require a lot of rethinking of how business works. Customer experience can become personalized, contextualized, and localized 24-7 for all your customers with the help of smart agents. The four Ps of marketing will need to adapt to fit a world that increasingly offers machine intelligence that can match human intelligence in many areas. Humans and machines will not only need to coexist; they will need to collaborate to win in the algorithmic economy in which data and algorithms will be the key to success. Today is the day to begin preparing for this future!

Notes

1 Robert Hetu, "New Research Highlights Algorithmic Business," Gartner Blog Network. Last modified March 15, 2016. http://blogs.gartner.com/robert-hetu/new-research-algorithmic-business/.

2 Eric Brynjolfsson and Andrew McAfee, *The Second Machine Age: Work, Progress, and Prosperity in a Time of Brilliant Technologies* (New York: Norton & Company, 2014).

3 Eric Schmidt and Jahen Cohen, *The New Digital Age: Reshaping the Future of People, Nations and Business* (London: John Murray Press, 2013), p. 6.

4 Schmidt and Cohen, *The New Digital Age*, p. 29.

5 Heather Levy, "Gartner Predicts Our Digital Future," Gartner Blog Network. Last modified October 6, 2015. http://www.gartner.com/newsroom/id/2866617.

6 Ibid.

7 Ibid.

8 Diffferent Strategieagentur, "The Programmatic Giant: Some Opportunities Are Too Big to Keep Secret," White Paper (2015).

9 Klaus Schwab, *The Fourth Industrial Revolution* (Geneva: World Economic Forum 2016).

10 David Ferrucci et al., "Building Watson: An Overview of the DeepQA Project," *AI Magazine* (Fall 2010).

11 Ferrucci, "Building Watson."

12 Rochelle Bilow, "We Spent a Year Cooking With the World's Smartest Computer—and Now You Can, Too," *Bon Appetit*, June 23, 2015. http://www.bonappetit.com/entertaining-style/trends-news/article/chef-watson-app.

13 IBM, "Watson Services." Last modified May 22, 2016. https://www.ibm.com/smarterplanet/us/en/ibmwatson/developercloud/services-catalog.html.

14 Automated Insights, "Automated Insights Is Revolutionizing the Way Professionals Create Content." Last modified May 18, 2016. https://automatedinsights.com/company/.

15 Automated Insights, "Wordsmith Platform in Action." Last modified May 18, 2016. https://automatedinsights.com/examples/.

16 Schmidt and Cohen, *The New Digital Age*, p. 4.

17 ComScore, "It's a Social World: Top 10 Need-to-Knows about Social Networking and Where It's Headed." Last modified December 21, 2011. http://www.comscore.com/Insights/Presentations-and-Whitepapers/2011/it_is_a_social_world_top_10_need-to-knows_about_social_networking.

18 Cara Pring, "216 Social Media and Internet Statistics (September 2012)," The Social Skinny. Last modified September 15, 2012. http://thesocialskinny.com/216-social-media-and-internet-statistics-september-2012/.

19 IBM, "Bringing Big Data to the Enterprise." Last modified May 18, 2016. http://www-01.ibm.com/software/data/bigdata/what-is-big-data.html.

20 IDC and EMC, "The Digital Universe of Opportunities: Rich Data and the Increasing Value of the Internet of Things." Last modified April 2014. http://www.emc.com/leadership/digital-universe/2014iview/internet-of-things.htm.

21 Neil Gershenfeld, Raffi Krikorian, and Danny Cohen, "The Internet of Things," *Scientific American* 291, no. 4 (1004): 76–81.

22 Schmidt and Cohen, *The New Digital Age*, p. 6.

23 "Computer Scientist Paris Smaragdis on 'Machine Listening,'" *MIT Technology Review*. Last modified October 11, 20=&. https://www.technologyreview.com/s/406664/computer-scientist-paris-smaragdis-on-machine-listening/.

24 Ravinder Dahiya and Maurizio Valle, *Robotic Tactile Sensing* (Amsterdam: Springer, 2013), p. 15.

25 Jason Dorrier, "Discover the Chemical Composition of Everyday Stuff… with a Smartphone Camera," Singularity Hub, April 17, 2015. http://singularityhub.com/2015/04/17/point-and-shoot-spectral-imaging-and-chemical-composition-with-a-smartphone-camera/.

26 Jason Dorrier, "Pen That Scans and Draws in Millions of Colors Finally Arrives on Kickstarter," Singularity Hub, August 12, 2014. http://singularityhub.com/2014/08/12/pen-that-scans-and-draws-in-millions-of-colors-finally-arrives-on-kickstarter/.

27 Marc Prosser, "Wearables Are Turning Your Pets and Other Animals into Big Data," Singularity Hub, December 30, 2015. http://singularityhub.com/2015/12/30/wearables-are-turning-your-pets-and-other-animals-into-big-data/.

28 Nelson Cowan, "What Are the Differences between Long-Term, Short-Term, and Working Memory?" *Progress in Brain Research* 169 (2008): 323–38. PMC. Web. January 17, 2016.

29 Daniel Kahneman, *Thinking, Fast and Slow* (New York: Macmillan, 2011).

30 Larry R. Squire, "Memory Systems of the Brain: A Brief History and Current Perspective," *Neurobiology of Learning and Memory* 82.3 (2004): 171–77.

31 American Psychological Association, "Glossary of Psychological Terms," (2013). Retrieved August 13, 2014. Apa.org.

32 You should go ahead and listen to Iamus's music yourself: http://www.bbc.com/future/story/20140808-music-like-never-heard-before.

33 *New York Times*, "*Times* Haiku—Serendipitous Poetry from the *New York Times*." Retrieved June 12, 2016. http://haiku.nytimes.com/.

34 Levy, "Gartner Predicts Our Digital Future."

35 Ibid.

36 George Westermann, Didier Bonnet, and Andrew McAfee, *Leading Digital: Turning Technology into Business Transformation* (New York: HBR Press, 2014), p. 30.

37 Daryl Travis with Harrison Yates, *How Does It Make You Feel? Why Emotion Wins the Battle of Brands* (Networlding Publishing, 2013).

38 Ibid.

39 Westermann et al., *Leading Digital*, p. 10l.

40 Adam Richardson, "Using Customer Journey Maps to Improve Customer Experience," *Harvard Business Review* (November 15, 2010). https://hbr.org/2010/11/using-customer-journey-maps-to/.

41 Westermann et al., *Leading Digital*, p. 34.

42 Keith Coe, "Transforming Your Organization into a Customer Experience Powerhouse," Forrester. Last modified April 19, 2016. http://blogs.forrester.com//keith_coe/16-04-19-transforming_your_organization_into_a_customer_experience_powerhouse.

43 Westermann et al., *Leading Digital*, p. 29.

44 The Federal Trade Commission (FTC) of the United States of America, "Protecting Consumer Privacy in an Era of Rapid Change," FTC Report (March 2012).

45 David Loshin and Abbie Reifer, *Using Information to Develop a Culture of Centricity: Customer Centricity, Analytics and Information Utilization* (Burlington, MA: Morgan Kaufmann Publishers, 2013), p. 3.

46 J. R. Bettman, M. F. Luce, and J. W. Payne, "Consumer Decision Making: A Constructive Perspective," in M. Tedeschi (ed.), *Consumer Behavior and Decision Making* (Berlin: Springer, 1991), pp. 1–42.

47 G. L. Lilien, P. Kotler, and S. K. Moorthy, *Marketing Models* (New York: Prentice Hall, 1992), pp. 22–23.

48 David Merrill and Reid Roger, *Personal Styles and Effective Performance* (Florida: CRC Press 1981).

49 Robert Bolton and Dorothy Glover Bolton, *Social Style/Management Style: Developing Productive Work Relationships* (New York: American Management Associations, 1984).

50 Alex Palmer, "Macy's Transformation," *Direct Marketing News*. Last modified April 1, 2012. http://www.dmnews.com/multichannel-marketing/macys-transformation/article/233631/.

51 Terry J. Lundgren, "Remarks by Terry J. Lundgren, Chairman and Chief Executive Officer, Macy's, Inc., to the 2014 Annual Meeting of Shareholders." Last modified May 16, 2014. https://www.macysinc.com/for-investors/chairmans-remarks/.

52 Jordan K. Speer, "Macy's Omnichannel Strategy on the Move," *Apparel Magazine*. Last modified May 12, 2012. http://apparel.edgl.com/news/macy-s-omni-channel-strategy-on-the-move80122.

53 Sarah Halzack, "Is the New Technology at Macy's Our First Glimpse of the Future of Retail?" *The Washington Post* (September 25, 2014).

54 Terry J. Lundgren, "Remarks by Terry J. Lundgren, Chairman and Chief Executive Officer, Macy's, Inc., to the 2014 Annual Meeting of Shareholders." Last modified May 16, 2014. https://www.macysinc.com/for-investors/chairmans-remarks/.

55 Starbucks Corporation, "Fiscal 2013 Annual Report" (November 18, 2013).

56 Stuart Lauchlan, "Drinking Starbucks's Digital Brew," *diginomica*. Last modified June 3, 2013. http://diginomica.com/2013/06/03/starbucks-digital-brew/.

57 Malcolm Wheatley, "Data-Driven Location Choices Drive Latest Starbucks Surge," Data Informed. Last modified January 10, 2013. http://data-informed.com/data-driven-location-choices-drive-latest-starbucks-surge/.

58 Starbucks.com, "Card Rewards." Retrieved October 24, 2010. http://www.starbucks.com/card/rewards.

59 David A. Kaplan, "Starbucks: The Art of Endless Transformation," *INC Magazine*. Last modified January 3, 2015. http://www.inc.com/magazine/201406/david-kaplan/howard-schultz-reinvents-starbucks-constantly.html.

60 Marcus Wohlsen, "Forget Apple Pay. The Master of Mobile Payments Is Starbucks," *WIRED*. Last modified March 11, 2014. http://www.wired.com/2014/11/forget-apple-pay-master-mobile-payments-starbucks/.

61 Michael Welch and Jerome Buvat, "Starbucks: Taking the 'Starbucks Experience' Digital," Cap Gemini Consulting Report, 2013.

62 Kate Kaye, "At Starbucks, Data Pours In—What to Do with It?" *Ad Age*. Last modified March 22, 2013. http://adage.com/article/datadriven-marketing/starbucks-data-pours/240502/.

63 Lauchlan, "Drinking Starbucks's Digital Brew."

64 Starbucks Corporation, "Fiscal 2013 Annual Report" (November 18, 2013).

65 Wohlsen, "Forget Apple Pay."

66 Welch and Buvat, "Starbucks: Taking the 'Starbucks Experience' Digital."

67 Mark McClusky, "The Nike Experiment: How the Shoe Giant Unleashed the Power of Personal Metrics," *WIRED* 22 (June 2009). Retrieved January 21, 2015. http://archive.wired.com/medtech/health/magazine/17-07/lbnp_nike?currentPage=all.

68 Scott Cendrowski, "Nike's New Marketing Mojo," *Fortune* (February 13, 2012). Retrieved January 21, 2015. http://fortune.com/2012/02/13/nikes-new-marketing-mojo/.

69 Austin Carr, "Nike: The No. 1 Most Innovative Company of 2013," *Fast Company Magazine.* Retrieved January 21, 2015. http://www.fastcompany.com/most-innovative-companies/2013/nike.

70 McClusky, "The Nike Experiment."

71 Samsung, "Connected Home: Getting Home Late." Retrieved May 22, 2016. http://techlife.samsung.com/getting-home-late-1368.html.

72 Airbus, "Applying Innovation to Improve the Airline Luggage Experience." Retrieved May 22, 2016. http://www.airbus.com/newsevents/news-events-single/detail/applying-innovation-to-improve-the-airline-luggage-experience/.

73 Peyman Azhari, Nilufar Faraby, Alexander Rossmann, Bernhard Steimel, and Kai S. Wichmann, "Digital Transformation Report 2014," Neuland GmbH & Co. KG (2014). Retrieved January 10, 2015. http://www.dt-award.de/download-center/.

74 IBM, "Vestas: Turning Climate into Capital with Big Data," IBM Smarter Planet (2011). Retrieved May 22, 2016. http://www-01.ibm.com/common/ssi/cgi-bin/ssialias?htmlfid=IMC14702USEN&appname=wwwsearch.

75 Ibid.

76 Ibid.

77 IBM, "Fighting Financial Money Laundering," IBM Smarter Planet (2010). Retrieved January 16, 2015. http://www-07.ibm.com/tw/dp-cs/smartbanking/pdf/ Case_Bancolombia_improves_suspicious_transaction_reporting_by_40_Bancolombia.PDF.

78 PriceWaterhouseCoopers, "2009 Global Economic Crime Survey," PricewaterhouseCoopers LLP (2009). Retrieved June 29, 2011. http://www.pwc.com/gx/en/economic-crime-survey.

79 IBM, "Fighting Financial Money Laundering."

80 Ibid.

81 Touch and Travel, "So funktioniert's." Retrieved May 22, 2016. https://www.touchandtravel.de/web/cupo/touchandtravel/funktionsweise.

82 Desire Athow, "Uber's Place in the Sharing Economy," *TechRadar* (January 18, 2015). Retrieved January 20, 2015. http://www.techradar.com/news/world-of-tech/uber-s-place-in-the-sharing-economy-1280948.

83 PYMNTS.com, "The Uber-Taxi Medallion Ripple Effect" (January 14, 2015). Retrieved January 20, 2015. http://www.pymnts.com/in-depth/2015/the-uber-taxi-medallion-ripple-effect/#.VL2QHi7F8VM.

84 Rob van der Meulen, "The Algorithm Economy Will Start a Huge Wave of Innovation," Gartner Blog Network, April 20, 2016. http://www.gartner.com/smarterwithgartner/the-algorithm-economy-will-start-a-huge-wave-of-innovation/.

85 D. Logan, J. King, and H. Fischer-Wright, *Tribal Leadership: Leveraging Natural Groups to Build a Thriving Organization* (Harper Collins, 2009).

86 ING, "The ING Way of Working." Retrieved June 6, 2016. https://www.ing.jobs/Netherlands/Why-ING/What-we-offer/Agile-working.htm.

87 Gartner, "Bimodal IT," June 6, 2016, http://www.gartner.com/it-glossary/bimodal/.

88 Heather Hinman, "The Do's and Don'ts of Data Mining," *KD Nuggets* (March 1, 2014). Retrieved January 26, 2015. http://www.kdnuggets.com/2014/03/data-mining-do-and-dont.html.

89 Shvetank Shah, Andrew Horne, and Jaime Capellá, "Good Data Won't Guarantee Good Decisions," *Harvard Business Review* (April 2012).

90 J. Weston Phippen, "How Toyota May Have Started Overcharging Minority Customers," *The Atlantic* (February 3, 2016). Retrieved May 5, 2016. http://www.theatlantic.com/business/archive/2016/02/toyota-car-loans-restitution/459678/.

91 Brynjolfsson and McAfee, *Race against the Machine*.

Bibliography

Airbus. "Applying innovation to improve the airline luggage experience." Retrieved May 22, 2016. http://www.airbus.com/newsevents/news-events-single/detail/applying-innovation-to-improve-the-airline-luggage-experience/.

American Psychological Association. "Glossary of Psychological Terms." 2013. Retrieved August 13, 2014. Apa.org.

Athow, Desire. "Uber's Place in the Sharing Economy." *TechRadar* (January 18, 2015). Retrieved January 20, 2015. http://www.techradar.com/news/world-of-tech/uber-s-place-in-the-sharing-economy-1280948.

Automated Insights. "Automated Insights Is Revolutionizing the Way Professionals Create Content." Last modified May 18, 2016. https://automatedinsights.com/company/.

Automated Insights. "Wordsmith Platform in Action." Last modified May 18, 2016. https://automatedinsights.com/examples/.

Azhari, Peyman, Nilufar Faraby, Alexander Rossmann, Bernhard Steimel, and Kai S. Wichmann. "Digital Transformation Report 2014." Neuland GmbH & Co. KG (2014). Retrieved January 10, 2015. http://www.dt-award.de/download-center/.

Bettman, J. R., M. F. Luce, and J. W. Payne. "Consumer Decision Making: A Constructive Perspective." In: Tedeschi, M., ed. *Consumer Behavior and Decision Making* (Berlin: Springer, 1991), 1–42.

Bilow, Rochelle. "We Spent a Year Cooking with the World's Smartest Computer—and Now You Can, Too." *Bon Appetit* (June 23, 2015).

http://www.bonappetit.com/entertaining-style/trends-news/article/chef-watson-app.

Bolton, Robert, and Dorothy Grover. *Social Style/Management Style: Developing Productive Work Relationships* (New York: American Management Associations, 1984).

Brynjolfsson, Erik, and Andrew McAfee. *Race Against the Machine* (Lexington, MA: Digital Frontier Press, 2011).

Brynjolfsson, Erik, and Andrew McAfee. *The Second Machine Age: Work, Progress, and Prosperity in a Time of Brilliant Technologies* (New York: Norton & Company, 2014).

Carr, Austin. "NIKE: The No. 1 Most Innovative Company of 2013." *Fast Company Magazine*. Retrieved January 21, 2015. http://www.fastcompany.com/most-innovative-companies/2013/nike.

Cendrowski, Scott. "Nike's New Marketing Mojo." *Fortune* (February 13, 2012). Retrieved January 21, 2015. http://fortune.com/2012/02/13/nikes-new-marketing-mojo/.

Coe, Keith. "Transforming Your Organization into a Customer Experience Powerhouse." Forrester. Last modified April 19, 2016. http://blogs.forrester.com//keith_coe/16-04-19-transforming_your_organization_into_a_customer_experience_powerhouse.

comScore. "It's a Social World: Top 10 Need-to-Knows About Social Networking and Where It's Headed." Last modified December 21, 2011. http://www.comscore.com/Insights/Presentations-and-Whitepapers/2011/it_is_a_social_world_top_10_need-to-knows_about_social_networking.

Cowan, Nelson. "What Are the Differences between Long-Term, Short-Term, and Working Memory?" *Progress in Brain Research* 169 (2008): 323–38. PMC. Web. January 17, 2016.

Dahiya, Ravinder, and Maurizio Valle. *Robotic Tactile Sensing* (Amsterdam: Springer, 2013), 15.

Diffferent Strategieagentur. "The Programmatic Giant: Some Opportunities Are Too Big to Keep Secret." White Paper (2015).

Dorrier, Jason. "Discover the Chemical Composition of Everyday Stuff… with a Smartphone Camera." Singularity Hub (April 17, 2015). http://singularityhub.com/2015/04/17/point-and-shoot-spectral-imaging-and-chemical-composition-with-a-smartphone-camera/.

Dorrier, Jason. "Pen That Scans and Draws in Millions of Colors Finally Arrives on Kickstarter." Singularity Hub (August 12, 2014). http://singularityhub.com/2014/08/12/pen-that-scans-and-draws-in-millions-of-colors-finally-arrives-on-kickstarter/.

The Federal Trade Commission (FTC) of the United States of America. "Protecting Consumer Privacy in an Era of Rapid Change." FTC Report (March 2012).

Ferrucci, David, et al. "Building Watson: An Overview of the DeepQA Project." *AI Magazine* (Fall 2010).

Gartner. "Bimodal IT" (June 6 2016). http://www.gartner.com/it-glossary/bimodal/.

Gershenfeld, Neil, Raffi Krikorian, and Danny Cohen. "The Internet of Things." *Scientific American* 291, no. 4 (1004): 76–81.

Halzack, Sarah. "Is the New Technology at Macy's Our First Glimpse of the Future of Retail?" *Washington Post* (September 25, 2014).

Hetu, Robert. "New Research Highlights Algorithmic Business." Gartner Blog Network. Last modified March 15, 2016. http://blogs.gartner.com/robert-hetu/new-research-algorithmic-business/.

Hinman, Heather. "The Do's and Don'ts of Data Mining." *KD Nuggets* (March 1, 2014). Retrieved January 26, 2015. http://www.kdnuggets.com/2014/03/data-mining-do-and-dont.html.

Hurwitz, Judith S., Marcia Kaufman, and Adrian Bowles. *Cognitive Computing and Big Data Analytics* (Indianapolis, IN: Wiley, 2015).

IBM. "Bringing Big Data to the Enterprise." Last modified May 18, 2016. http://www-01.ibm.com/software/data/bigdata/what-is-big-data.html.

IBM. "Fighting Financial Money Laundering." *IBM Smarter Planet* (2010). Retrieved January 16, 2015. http://www-07.ibm.com/tw/dp-cs/smart-banking/pdf/ Case_Bancolombia_improves_suspicious_transaction_ reporting_by_40_Bancolombia.PDF.

IBM. "Vestas: Turning Climate into Capital with Big Data." *IBM Smarter Planet* (2011). Retrieved May 22, 2016. http://www-01.ibm.com/common/ssi/cgi-bin/ssialias?htmlfid=IMC14702USEN&appname=wwwsearch.

IBM. "Watson Services." Last modified May 22, 2016. https://www.ibm.com/smarterplanet/us/en/ibmwatson/developercloud/services-catalog.html.

IDC and EMC. "The Digital Universe of Opportunities: Rich Data and the Increasing Value of the Internet of Things." Last modified April 2014.

http://www.emc.com/leadership/digital-universe/2014iview/internet-of-things.htm.

ING. "The ING way of working." Retrieved June 6, 2016. https://www.ing.jobs/Netherlands/Why-ING/What-we-offer/Agile-working.htm.

Kahneman, Daniel. *Thinking, Fast and Slow* (New York: Macmillan, 2011).

Kaplan, David A. "Starbucks: The Art of Endless Transformation." *INC Magazine*. Last modified January 3, 2015. http://www.inc.com/magazine/201406/david-kaplan/howard-schultz-reinvents-starbucks-constantly.html.

Kaye, Kate. "At Starbucks, Data Pours In—What to Do with It?" *Ad Age*. Last modified March 22, 2013. http://adage.com/article/datadriven-marketing/starbucks-data-pours/240502/.

Lauchlan, Stuart. "Drinking Starbucks's Digital Brew." *diginomica*. Last modified June 3, 2013. http://diginomica.com/2013/06/03/starbucks-digital-brew/.

Levy, Heather. "Gartner Predicts Our Digital Future." Gartner Blog Network. Last modified October 6, 2015. http://www.gartner.com/newsroom/id/2866617.

Lilien, G. L., P. Kotler, and S. K. Moorthy. *Marketing Models* (New York: Prentice Hall, 1992), 22–23.

Logan, D., J. King, and H. Fischer-Wright. *Tribal Leadership: Leveraging Natural Groups to Build a Thriving Organization* (Harper Collins, 2009).

Loshin, David, and Abbie Reifer. *Using Information to Develop a Culture of Centricity: Customer Centricity, Analytics and Information Utilization* (Burlington, MA: Morgan Kaufmann Publishers, 2013), 3.

Lundgren, Terry J. "Remarks by Terry J. Lundgren, Chairman and Chief Executive Officer, Macy's, Inc., to the 2014 Annual Meeting of Shareholders." Last modified May 16, 2014. https://www.macysinc.com/for-investors/chairmans-remarks/.

McClusky, Mark. "The Nike Experiment: How the Shoe Giant Unleashed the Power of Personal Metrics." *WIRED* 22 (June 2009). Retrieved January 21, 2015. http://archive.wired.com/medtech/health/magazine/17-07/lbnp_nike?currentPage=all.

Merrill, David, and Reid Roger. *Personal Styles & Effective Performance* (Florida: CRC Press, 1981).

MIT Technology Review. "Computer Scientist Paris Smaragdis on 'Machine Listening.'" Last modified October 11, 2016. https://www.technologyreview.com/s/406664/computer-scientist-paris-smaragdis-on-machine-listening/.

New York Times. "*Times* Haiku—Serendipitous Poetry from the *New York Times*." Retrieved June 12, 2016. http://haiku.nytimes.com/.

Nourbakhsh, Illah Reza. *Robot Futures* (Cambridge, MA: MIT Press, 2013).

Palmer, Alex. "Macy's Transformation." *Direct Marketing News*. Last modified April 1, 2012. http://www.dmnews.com/multichannel-marketing/macys-transformation/article/233631/.

Phippen, J. Weston. "How Toyota May Have Started Overcharging Minority Customers." *The Atlantic* (February 3, 2016). Retrieved

May 5, 2016. http://www.theatlantic.com/business/archive/2016/02/toyota-car-loans-restitution/459678/.

PriceWaterhouseCoopers. "2009 Global Economic Crime Survey." PriceWaterhouseCoopers LLP (2009). Retrieved June 29, 2011. http://www.pwc.com/gx/en/economic-crime-survey.

Pring, Cara. "216 Social Media and Internet Statistics (September 2012)." *The Social Skinny.* Last modified September 15, 2012. http://thesocial-skinny.com/216-social-media-and-internet-statistics-september-2012/.

Prosser, Marc. "Wearables Are Turning Your Pets and Other Animals into Big Data." Singularity Hub (December 30, 2015). http://singularityhub.com/2015/12/30/wearables-are-turning-your-pets-and-other-animals-into-big-data/.

PYMNTS.com. "The Uber-Taxi Medallion Ripple Effect" (January 14, 2015). Retrieved January 20, 2015. http://www.pymnts.com/in-depth/2015/the-uber-taxi-medallion-ripple-effect/#.VL2QHi7F8VM.

Richardson, Adam. "Using Customer Journey Maps to Improve Customer Experience." *Harvard Business Review* (November 15, 2010). https://hbr.org/2010/11/using-customer-journey-maps-to/.

Samsung. "Connected Home: Getting Home Late." Retrieved May 22, 2016. http://techlife.samsung.com/getting-home-late-1368.html.

Schmidt, Eric, and Jahen Cohen. *The New Digital Age: Reshaping the Future of People, Nations and Business* (London: John Murray Press, 2013).

Schwab, Klaus. *The Fourth Industrial Revolution* (Geneva: World Economic Forum 2016).

Shah, Shvetank, Andrew Horne, and Jaime Capellá. "Good Data Won't Guarantee Good Decisions." *Harvard Business Review* (April 2012).

Speer, Jordan K. "Macy's Omnichannel Strategy on the Move." *Apparel Magazine*. Last modified May 12, 2012. http://apparel.edgl.com/news/macy-s-omni-channel-strategy-on-the-move80122.

Squire, Larry R. "Memory Systems of the Brain: A Brief History and Current Perspective." *Neurobiology of Learning and Memory* 82.3 (2004): 171–77.

Starbucks Corporation. Fiscal 2013 Annual Report (November 18, 2013).

Starbucks.com. "Card Rewards." Retrieved October 24, 2010. http://www.starbucks.com/card/rewards.

Touch and Travel. "So funktioniert's." Retrieved May 22, 2016. https://www.touchandtravel.de/web/cupo/touchandtravel/funktionsweise.

Travis, Daryl, with Harrison Yates. *How Does It Make You Feel? Why Emotion Wins the Battle of Brands* (Networlding Publishing, 2013).

Van der Meulen, Rob. "The Algorithm Economy Will Start a Huge Wave of Innovation." Gartner Blog Network (April 20, 2016). http://www.gartner.com/smarterwithgartner/the-algorithm-economy-will-start-a-huge-wave-of-innovation/.

Van der Meulen, Rob. "When Smart Things Rule the World." Gartner Blog Network. Last modified August 14, 2015. http://www.gartner.com/smarterwithgartner/when-smart-things-rule-the-world/.

Welch, Michael, and Jerome Buvat. "Starbucks: Taking the 'Starbucks Experience' Digital." Cap Gemini Consulting Report, 2013.

Westermann, George, Didier Bonnet, and Andrew McAfee. *Leading Digital: Turning Technology into Business Transformation* (New York: HBR Press, 2014).

Wheatley, Malcolm. "Data-Driven Location Choices Drive Latest Starbucks Surge." Data Informed. Last modified January 10, 2013. http://data-informed.com/data-driven-location-choices-drive-latest-starbucks-surge/.

Wohlsen, Marcus. "Forget Apple Pay. The Master of Mobile Payments Is Starbucks." *WIRED*. Last modified March 11, 2014. http://www.wired.com/2014/11/forget-apple-pay-master-mobile-payments-starbucks/.

www.ingramcontent.com/pod-product-compliance
Lightning Source LLC
Chambersburg PA
CBHW080617190526
45169CB00009B/3214